Planned Giving Basics

THE WHY, THE WHO, AND THE HOW

Books by Carol Weisman, MSW, CSP

- *Becoming One of the Grateful Dead: Where There's a Will, There's a Way*, publication date Fall 2018
- *Transforming Ordinary People into Fundraising Superheroes... Even Those Who Hate to Ask*
- *Raising Charitable Children*
- *Losing your Executive Director Without Losing Your Way*, Carol Weisman and Richard Goldbaum
- *The Business Professional's Guide to Nonprofit Board Service*, Charles F. Damback, Oliver Tessier and Carol Weisman
- *Secrets of Successful Retreats: The Best from the Nonprofit Pros*
- *Secrets of Successful Fundraising: The Best from the Nonprofit Pros*
- *Build a Better Board in 30 Days*
- *A Corporate Employee's Guide to Nonprofit Board Service*

Planned Giving Basics

THE WHY, THE WHO, AND THE HOW

Carol Weisman MSW, CSP

F. E. Robbins & Sons Press

Saint Louis MO

*To Dianne Belk, champion for the Girl Scouts,
who was my first client since I launched Board Builders in 1994
to ask for a planned gift. I said "yes."*

*And to my son Jono Robbins
When Jono was two and wanted something, we'd ask,
"What is the magic word?" and Jono would growl: "NOW!"*

*In fact, my darling son, the magic words are:
"Will you join me and thank you."*

Planned Giving Basics, The Why, the Who, and the How
© 2018 Carol Weisman. All rights reserved.

This book may not be duplicated in any way without the express written consent of the author, except in the case of brief excerpts or quotations for the purpose of review. No part of this book may be reproduced or transmitted in any form or by any means (electronic, mechanical, photographic, recordings, or otherwise) without the prior permission of the author. The information contained herein is for the personal use of the reader and may not be incorporated in any commercial programs or other books, databases, or any kind of software without the written consent of the author. Making copies of this book or any portion of it for any purpose is a violation of the United States copyright laws.

ISBN: 978-0-9992332-0-7
Cartoons by Dennis Fletcher
Cover and interior design: n-kcreative.com

Printed in the United States of America
Published by

F.E. Robbins & Sons Press

St. Louis, MO • BoardBuilders.com • carol@boardbuilders.com

Contents

Preface: Why are my favorite charities in my estate plan?......1

Introduction: Word challenges 3

1. Why bother with planned giving......7

2. Why do people make planned gifts......31

3. Who to ask......47

4. How to research your donors......73

5. How to ask......89

6. Who should make the ask......119

7. How to bring up the subject of a planned gift......139

8. How to steward your donors......171

9. How to market your planned giving program......191

10. What are you going to ask for......213

11. Policies and procedures......241

12. The power phrases that pay......259

Acknowledgments......263

The Change Maker's Cheer

Stand up and raise your arms above your head
(like the Y in the song *YMCA*)
I aspire

Now put your hands over your heart and stand
up straight and proud
To Inspire

Slump down, arms limp at your side
Until I Expire

Adapted from a quote from my mentor
Jerry Horowitz who can't remember
where he originally heard it.

PREFACE

Why are my favorite charities in my estate plan?

I like to give.

My parents were both affluent and generous and, therefore, able to give us a good life. I never wanted for anything (other than a cure for cellulite). I believe that I am "paying it backward" for the blessings I've received. It makes me feel good to give. I consider myself more an egotist than a philanthropist.

The best gift I have ever given was a small one. I was working in Texas with my colleague Michael Daigneault. Michael has a serious Diet Coke habit. I have a mild Diet Pepsi habit. I asked one of the servers who was setting up breakfast if we could get some diet sodas. She asked how many. Michael said "five," and I said "one." She came back with six cans of soda. During the day, she checked in and asked if we needed more. I had a second Diet Pepsi. After lunch, a supervisor asked where we got the diet sodas. When we told her that the waitress had brought them, she smiled and said, "That figures." She then explained that soda in cans were only available in the employees' lounge. The waitress was paying for them herself. At the end of the day, I gave the waitress a $100 tip. She thought it was a mistake and, in halting English, tried to return it. I was incredibly touched by her generosity and her honesty. Giving her that tip felt great.

My mother always said that charity starts at home. I want my son Jono, who is a hard-working high school art teacher, to have his lake cottage with a boat, and I want my son Frank and his wife, Laura, to be able to travel and relax while their three sons, Frank, Tommy, and Eli, go to college on an Oma and Opa (that's us!) scholarship. But there is a lot more to life that I want, which I can accomplish neither alone nor in my lifetime. That is why I give today and why my favorite charities are in my estate plan. I don't miss the money, and, more importantly, I don't plan to die!

Introduction

Word Challenges

When writing this book, I faced several issues regarding the choice of words to use. The first was the importance of being politically correct vs. being understood. As to political correctness, some people perceive the word "charity" as pejorative. It is used in the names of many old nonprofits such as Catholic Charities as well as in younger organizations such as Charity Navigator, an independent charity watchdog organization founded in 2001. I have chosen to use the terms "nonprofit" and "organization" with only a sprinkling of the term "charity" to describe a 501(c)(3), which is simply a tax code. Outside the U.S. these organizations are referred to as NGOs or Non-Governmental Organizations. I feared that throwing in the term NGO would muddy the waters even more.

I define a planned gift as any gift made in the donor's lifetime or at death as part of a donor's estate plan.

A second challenge was what to name the book. When I told people that I was writing a book on "planned giving" they would say, "Oh, you mean 'bequests.'" Well, not all planned gifts are bequests. Another term that is not commonly used is "deferred giving." Older folks, primarily those over 80, are more familiar with this terminology. Younger people, however, thought it meant a major gift donated over many years.

I also struggled with how to describe the document that outlines one's final charitable wishes. The most common terms are estate plans, legacy gifts, wills, and trusts. I went for broke and use these terms interchangeably, although there are slight differences.

For 24 years, I have argued with my dear friend and colleague Susan Ellis, founder of Energizer Inc., about differentiating between the terms "volunteer" and "board member." Both are usually unpaid. (Less than one percent of nonprofit board members are compensated.) Board members usually have a commitment of two to three years of service and, with term limits, can be on a board for a limited number of years. A volunteer has much more flexibility and can say "yes" to anything from a "one and done," a two-week mission trip, or volunteering every Wednesday for 50 years. The most important point I have learned from Susan is that the term "volunteer" is a pay category and not a job description. You can be an electrician or physician, a boy scout or girl scout, or a felon ordered to community service. You can be under 10 or over 80. You can perform any task for which you are qualified or willing to get training. This might mean planting trees, feeding the poor, or repairing a cleft palate. So, when I use the term "board member" I am speaking of a specific type of volunteer role that requires moral, legal, and financial commitment to a specific organization for a specific time. The work of a board member is governance rather than management and, frequently, the insurance of financial resources, that is, fundraising.

And finally, how to describe the person making the gift? Is that person a donor, a giver, or a philanthropist? Middle-class people are more comfortable with the terms "donor" and "giver." Even Warren Buffet does not consider himself a philanthropist, although many who have given far less do use that term when describing themselves. I decided to use the words "donor" and "giver." If you are giving an amount that makes you consider yourself a philanthropist, I apologize and thank you.

THINK STRATEGICALLY WHEN CREATING YOUR FUNDRAISING PLAN.

1

Why bother with planned giving

It's all about the numbers

Here is a shocking fact: Dead people give more than corporations. Since Giving USA began tracking the sources of charitable gifts in 1975, non-profits have received more funding from bequests than from corporate giving in every year except one (1984). Moreover, while the total dollar amount of corporate and estate giving used to be roughly equal, the value of bequests began to pull steadily ahead in the 1990s and over the last decade has continually outpaced corporate donations by about 60 percent.

To provide incentive and backup for how to spend your time and money on fundraising, here are the actual numbers from the most reliable source in the U.S.

Giving USA: 2017 Charitable Giving

Where the $390 billion donated comes from:
- Bequests 9%
- Corporations 5%
- Individuals 71%
- Foundations 6%

Where the donations go:
- 32% Religion
- 15% Education
- 12% Human Services
- 10% Foundations
- 8% Health
- 8% Public-Society Benefit
- 6% International Affairs
- 5% Arts, Culture and Humanities
- 3% Environment/Animals
- 2% Individuals

This is only a partial look at giving in America. According to the Pew Research Center, in 2015 new immigrant Americans sent an estimated $582 billion to relatives in their home countries. The pattern of coming to America, earning money, and sending it to family back home is certainly not new. In 1947, my mother immigrated to the U.S. from Germany. She sent money to her sisters and brothers. When Germany began to once again thrive, she could focus on charitable causes closer to home. People in America typically prioritize their spending: first, taking care of themselves; second, taking care of their families; and third, giving to charity.

The numbers change from year to year, but the differences tend to be minor. I recommend looking at Giving USA's annual report. It contains a ton of useful data, which is great for benchmarking. One of my clients couldn't believe that the segment he volunteered in received only 3% of the giving pie. He named one of the larger organizations in the field, with a total budget of around $15 million. I mentioned Harvard and BJC Healthcare, a nonprofit and the largest employer in the state of Missouri, and he began to understand how vast the sector is and how large some of the "big dogs" can be. He also realized that, because of the competition, he was going to have to give more and raise more to make his nonprofit sustainable.

There are, of course, exceptions. If you have a disease-related charity in New Jersey, you might bring in a large portion of your contributions from corporations, because many of the largest pharmaceutical companies are based there. The most consistently savvy nonprofit board members and staff I have ever worked with are in Indiana, where the Eli Lilly pharmaceutical company is headquartered. The Lilly Endowment is dedicated to education and community development, and its first geographical priority is to the people of Indiana.

For your organization, planned giving not only reaps more long-term benefits for your organization but is more cost-effective. In *The Complete Guide to*

Fundraising Management, 4th Edition, authors Stanley Weinstein and Pamela Barden, inspired by the work of James M. Greenfield, drive home this point.

Fundraising Method	Typical Expense Range
Direct Mail Acquisition	$1.25 to $1.50 per $ raised
Direct Mail Renewal	$ 0.02 to $.25 per $ raised
E-Appeals	$ 0.04 per $ raised
Special Events	$ 0.20 per $ raised
Grants: Corporation and Foundation	$ 0.20 per $ raised
Planned Giving	$ 0.25 per $ raised
Major Gift Personal Solicitation Programs	$ 0.05 to $0.10 per $ raised
Capital Campaigns	$ 0.05 to $0.10 per $ raised
Reprinted with permission *The Complete Guide to Fundraising Management* by Stanley Weinstein and Pamela Barden, Wiley, 2017	

According to the software company Blackbaud, "Once a planned giving program is established, nonprofits can expect a cost of 3¢ to 15¢ per each $1 raised. This cost-to-donation ratio is important, not only to the organization but also to the donors who want their gifts to make a difference in the world rather than to be spent on additional fundraising efforts. Historically, planned gifts have increased nearly 5% every year, even during recessions, while other sources of revenue decline in times of economic struggle." I believe that we continue to want to give even during recessions because our family and friends might be going through a rough time.

Just think about your own personal resources. Do you have the most money in:
- Cash?
- Real estate?
- Other investments such as stocks and bonds?
- Insurance policies?

Most of us have the least amount in cash. In fact, only 10% of the wealth in the U.S. is in cash. When you ask for a cash gift, even if it is quite large, for most Americans it will not be as much as you will get in a planned gift. One of the planned giving professionals I met at a conference said, "If all you are getting is cash, you are leaving money on the table."

Again, I realize that you need money today, so ask for both. This is known as a blended gift, meaning some funds will transfer during the donor's lifetime and some after. For instance, one donor wanted to live out her life on her farm. She had several buildings on the farm that she wanted to give to a nonprofit that works with female victims of human trafficking. She gave the entire farm to the nonprofit with the provision that she could live her life in her home. At her death, the nonprofit would receive her entire portfolio, provided the nonprofit would continue to serve the same population. For giving the land, the donor got credit from both the nonprofit and the IRS. She had no living relatives that she liked, and she enjoyed having the women live on her property. She taught them English as a second language, while they taught her how to grow crops from their native countries.

There is a big push at many nonprofits to involve millennials, many of whom have been volunteering since high school or earlier. When many of us went to college in the '60s and '70s, there was no section on our applications to list volunteer work. Today, it is typically expected for admission.

When it comes to donors, however, it's another story. Young Americans have greater debt than ever before. The average graduate of the class of 2016 has more than $37,000 in student loan debt, up 6% from the previous year. In total, Americans carry more than $1.4 trillion in student loan debt. What this means is that young people are taking longer to get into the housing market and accumulate wealth, thereby hindering their ability to give financially to their favorite causes. My friend and mentor Simone Bernstein, age 23, told me that she was born in a digital land and that I am a tourist. Too true.

Ask millennials for their time and digital support and be thrilled when donations also come your way.

How much should you ask for? The average charitable bequest gift in the U.S. ranges from $35,000 to $70,000. This figure is not a one-size-fits-all proposition, however, which is why research and strategy are critical.

Rule of thumb:

- A planned giving target gift amount is 200 times a donor's largest gift

$1,000 = $200,000 (www.plannedgiving.com, 2017)

- A donor must give 20 times their current gift to endow their annual gift (assumes a 5% payout from the endowment fund)

$1,000 = $20,000

Remember: Thumbs are different sizes and the numbers can lie or be misleading. I remember once being asked to join a nonprofit board. When I asked what the average gift was, the recruiting board member said, "$45,000." I quickly took two steps back. This amount was way more than we could afford. We had two sons in college, and neither my husband nor I had a trust fund. But I had asked the wrong question. I should have asked for the mean. The recruiting board member forgot to mention that one family gave $1 million. So I did not have the optimum information to decide. Once I had the information, I joined. Keep the size of different thumbs in mind when estimating your gifts.

Real estate value is a big factor. If your nonprofit is bequeathed a mid-century modern, 1800-square-foot ranch house in La Jolla, California, the value will be astronomically different than the same size ranch house in Hannibal, Missouri. After a number of years, you will discover the average number and size of your gifts, and you can do some rough planning. You can and should ask your legacy donors how much they assume you will receive, but the numbers can be quite inaccurate, and some people don't want to disclose the amount. A widow in San Francisco left various charities a total of $750,000, each getting $150,000. The problem was that her house was worth $450,000. The other residents of her gentrified neighborhood had put hundreds of thousands into their homes. Her kitchen hadn't been updated since the 1950s avocado green and harvest yellow era. The charities spent a lot of money on lawyers, but the fair market value was $450,000. The house was her only asset.

Another challenge to accuracy is that much of the data is gathered through the IRS. If you give $20 for Girl Scout cookies to be sent to our military troops, drop money in the collection box at a museum or your place of worship, or write many small checks to your favorite charities, but you do not itemize on your tax form, your gifts are not calculated in yearly totals. Therefore, the actual amount that people give is much higher than the statistics indicate.

I know what some of you who work for nonprofits might be thinking:

- We need money today, not in 10 years. If we don't get money in the door today, and I mean *today*, we can't launch our next concert, feed our homeless, or keep teens productively occupied so that they don't join a gang. And don't forget paying our staff. And then there is the electric bill.

- We have a small staff and don't have the bandwidth to take on another fundraising project.
- Our board is barely involved in fundraising, and when members come up with an idea, it is a staff-intensive special event. As if we don't have enough golf tournaments, trivia nights, and galas in our town already.
- Our board is not thinking of what our community needs will be 10-20 years into the future.
- We have one board member who is always talking about a grand plan that would require $20 million for a new building when our largest gift to date has been $5,000. (His last gift was $250.) He refers to himself as a visionary. The staff has other names for him.
- If we do start a planned giving program, how can I get recognition if these people don't die while I'm here? The "major gifts people" just keep raking in the dough.
- How am I going to talk to people about what happens after their death? What kind of conversation is that to have with a stranger?

If any of these issues are your day-to-day reality, this chapter can help your staff and board to get started. If these aren't your issues, this information might be the ammo you need to answer questions on why now might not be the time to launch a full-blown planned giving program. It is not unheard of for board members to say something like, "My university got $73 million in planned gifts this year.

Why aren't we doing more in planned giving?" Reasonable question, except this university has 300 people in the development department while the board he sits on has three, which includes the data-entry dude. Plus, your organization was founded four years ago. His university is 123 years old.

If you have a vibrant planned giving program, this chapter will help you explain to new board and staff why it is so vital for your long-term survival and thrival.

Other fundraising options to consider

Hopefully, you don't have all your assets in one place. For instance, if all your stock was in Warren Buffett's company Berkshire Hathaway, you made out well. If the bulk of your estate was in Enron or you were a partner in now-defunct Arthur Andersen, not so good. If you have all your money in a house or boat or business, again, things can change on a dime. That is why financial advisors recommend diversifying your portfolio.

You should diversify your fundraising techniques as well. You must weigh risk, opportunity, and the status of your organization in terms of needs. Planned giving might be a crucial aspect of your overall strategy for sustainable funding, but it should never be your only method.

If you have been in the fundraising field for years, skip this section. This is for folks who are either passionate about and/or experts in a specific area and have little to no fundraising experience and would benefit from an overview of methodologies. When asked to chair a board, put their hat in the ring to be the executive director, or decides to found a nonprofit, many lawyers, educators, scientists, artists, social workers, etc., are either patrons of the organization or experts in their fields but have little knowledge of how to best raise a dollar.

Two scenarios for planned giving outcomes

A development director at a prep school landed a bequest of $5 million his first week on the job. It turned out that 23 years earlier one of his predecessors had asked for the gift. The new development director's goal was $2 million for the year. Obviously, at the end of his first week, he was a happy and optimistic camper. It is important to note that the elite school was founded in 1810 and tuition is high.

Compare this development professional at a venerable boarding school to his counterpart who is one of only three paid staff (after the executive director and an administrative assistant) for an organization that is three years old and has 75 donor names on an Excel spread sheet. Average gift: $43. What are the chances of getting a planned gift of $1000, much less $5 million? As they say on the TV ads: "Results may vary." This organization is not ready to expend a great deal of time or effort on planned giving. Donors want to know that the organization is going to survive before they make a planned gift. This is the time to look for other sources of funding, such as individual giving, grants, fee for services, and special events.

Expectations for other fundraising techniques

With capital campaigns, if you include staff time, the numbers change dramatically. A president, CEO, or executive director might spend 50% or more of his or her time on a capital campaign. If you include their salary, the staff member setting up meetings, funds for donor search software, and other development staff salaries, you are looking at a much different net number. And these expenses don't include outside counsel for a feasibility study, the actual campaign plan, or the marketing materials. If you are creating a national or international campaign, travel might be another expense. When you ask how much was raised and are told $8 million, you might want to ask if that includes staff time. It is rarely included. The average cost for expenses such as fundraising counsel, marketing, etc., is 4% to 10% of the average capital campaign revenue. The larger, older, and more sophisticated the organization, the lower the percentage, because the staff is already trained, systems are in place, and donors have been identified.

Many capital campaigns include an endowment portion. This is a great place to ask for a planned gift. Or, if your capital campaign goes well and doesn't include an endowment, follow up with another thank you, an update on progress, and a request for a planned gift. You already know this person cares about your organization. I had a client who was reluctant to "go back to the well," as he phrased it. I suggested he call all his donors, both large and small, thank them for what they had done, tell them the state of the organization, and share with them that he had made a planned gift and that he would not ask them for one more penny while they were alive. He explained that to continue the great work they started together, there needed to be funding for generations to come. He was dumbfounded when people joyfully said "yes" to a planned gift. In the two years that followed the planned gift request, the client sent the donors progress updates, and checks continued to come in.

With an increase in planned gifts, smaller organizations might anticipate a 10% or greater drop in annual giving. Better-staffed organizations have the bandwidth to continue to ask and steward donors during a campaign for annual fund gifts.

Corporate Giving

Why don't corporations give more? You might have heard rants in your boardroom that such and such corporation has plenty of money and should be giving more. If it is a publicly traded corporation, its responsibility is to its shareholders, who reap the profits and are then able to do what they want. They can give it to charity, put kids through school, retile the swimming pool, etc. If it is a privately held corporation, again, the shareholders may get to decide what happens to the profits from their investment.

Ideally, the corporation should take what has been called "The Janus Approach" to giving. Janus is the mythological Roman god typically depicted as having two faces, looking both to the future and to the past. When applied to corporate giving, Janus represents looking with one face to the corporation and one face to the community. So ideally, if you are a corporation that needs more engineers, fund engineering scholarships. If your employees need day care, that is where your charitable dollars should go. The arts enrich the lives of all employees. Giving to health care ensures a healthy work force. And so on.

If you are looking for sponsorships, corporations are the hot ticket. The closer they are aligned with your mission, the easier it will be. If you are Ralston Purina and make puppy chow, for example, animal rescue organizations are a great fit. If you are a brokerage firm and want to appeal to art collectors, sponsoring an art installation at a local museum to which you invite your current and potential clients is a smart business affiliation.

Sometimes it is the personal life of the CEO that can lead you to a sponsorship. If your nonprofit is dedicated to eradicating childhood diseases and the CEO has a child with asthma, you are likely to get a sponsorship even if the CEO's company makes plumbing fixtures. This is particularly true if it is a privately held company. The best way to get a sponsorship is to read—in its entirety— the company's website.

There are multiple paths into a corporation. They include: getting the attention of the CEO; applying to the foundation, if there is one; working with sales or marketing. The least amount of money is in the foundation. If you are looking for talent rather than funds, start with the human resources department.

If there is a personal letter or blog from the CEO, quote from that when going to the director of marketing or sales. The director of marketing at your local bank, factory, or other for-profit corporation will know that you did your homework when you share the CEO's statement that community engagement is their priority. A match made in nonprofit heaven! There is also a quid pro quo when it comes to both corporate and individual giving. If a company's major client wants a donation to a favorite charity and asks for a corporate gift, the gift has a good chance of being given. Vendors from food service companies to law firms are accustomed to being asked for charitable contributions with the backing of the C-Suite and other powerful decision makers. Likewise, there is a certain amount of check swapping at every level. You give to my charity, and I give to yours. Therefore, boards seek people of affluence and influence, where the check swapping is at a higher level.

Some regulated agencies must give funds back to the community. The Community Reinvestment Act (CRA) instructs the appropriate federal financial supervisory agencies to encourage regulated financial institutions to help meet the credit needs of the local communities in which they are chartered. To enforce the statute, federal regulatory agencies examine banking institutions for CRA compliance and take their findings into consideration when approving applications for new bank branches or for mergers and acquisitions. If you have a board member with a lot of money, either corporate or personal, in a specific financial institution, that board member should be asking on behalf of your nonprofit. Having the decision-maker from the financial institution on your board is also a smart nonprofit move—it cuts out the middleman.

Direct mail

Results are very different based on what kind of an organization you are. For instance, if you are an educational institution with good records, you have a natural constituency. If your mission is focused on a rare disease, you might have better results searching chat rooms on the Internet because of HIPPA, which comprises non-disclosure laws. The age of your organization and the age of your donors will also determine your yield. The longer your donors have been giving through direct mail solicitation, the greater the chances that they will continue if you steward them properly.

And of course, you must have the right information told in the best possible way to appeal to your supporters. Direct mail is part art and part science.

According to marketing guru James Lawrence, "Too many nonprofits have their priorities backwards. They spend 80 percent of their time and resources courting the 80 percent of donors who will give them 20 percent of their funding. And then they do very little to keep their newly acquired donors. It's not smart to do expensive donor acquisition, then lose eight out of 10 new donors because you don't steward them effectively. Bottom line: It's more cost-effective to retain a donor than to acquire a new one."

Getting that second gift from a donor can be hard, but when nonprofits invest their time in forming the bond needed to get that next gift, they open the door to a lifetime of giving from that supporter.

Many years ago, I worked with a board member of a child abuse agency who wrote a letter to 100 friends and colleagues. This was the first time she disclosed her horrific history of physical and psychological abuse. We are talking being chained in a shed for 24-hour periods and worse. She had a 68% response rate and was furious with the 32% who decided not to send a check. I tried to explain that a 10% response would have been fantastic; a 68% rate was through the roof. I brought in a bunch of books on direct mail (this was pre-Internet) to convince her of her success. You have to manage expectations.

This over-the-top response came from a single letter. You will need to create a plan that is more than a single touch. Some of this woman's friends thought it might be a sick joke and that it couldn't possibly be true. One impression or once-a-year letter won't get the job done.

Again, it doesn't cost a penny to add a line about planned giving with specific language on how to make the gift and who to contact for more information.

Special events

They can cost far more or far less than the national average of 50 cents per dollar of their total gross proceeds. Again, most organizations do not include staff time. If they did, you might find the figure closer to 80 cents per dollar spent on expenses. On the other hand, a large organization such as a university or place of worship might already have catering services or special events professionals on staff, with little or no cost for rentals, liquor license (if you need or want one), and other expenses. Also, some special events are hosted by generous donors who pay for the food and drink. The staff might be responsible for invitations and thank-you notes, but when you include staff time you wind up with an event costing more like 5% to 10% of gross proceeds.

Many events have a program book. This is a place where you can share planned giving opportunities, and, if you have a legacy society, you can feature its members with their permission.

Fee for service

This is another form of income. Educational institutions, hospitals, arts organizations, and many others charge for their services. The challenge is that the price might not cover the total cost, so if you are looking for diversity, experimental programs, top facilities, and a competitive edge, you must rely on philanthropy.

Let your donors know what the real cost is and what they can do to continue the services they are receiving with a planned gift. One independent school headmaster I worked with explained in a financial report the actual cost of educating a student per year, compared to the tuition that families were paying. A bit of a wag, he concluded his annual appeal in bold type: "When you lose $1,235 per student per year, you can't make up the difference in volume. I learned that from Mrs. Myers in fifth-grade math when I was a student here. Please join me as a legacy donor so that Mrs. Myers' teaching will not have been in vain and our children and grandchildren will benefit from our unique approach to education."

Government funding

Whether state or federal, this type of funding can be dicey. It might vanish one year with the stroke of a pen.

A wildlife sanctuary in the western U.S. lost $90,000 of Environmental Protection Agency money with little notice. The sanctuary's total budget was $350,000, so this loss was a major hit. An organization that provides services to adults with developmental disabilities has not had a pay increase in nine years. Another client that provides home heating got an incredible boon in the Obama years using government dollars for solar energy.

The next election cycle, funding was eliminated, people lost their jobs, and several nonprofits went under. You just don't know what funding will suddenly disappear or become available, which makes budgeting difficult. Plus, between the cost of grant writing expertise and the collection of data and staff time spent writing reports, applying for government funding can be a nightmare. I am not saying that relying on planned giving is reliable. It, too, can be erratic and labor-intensive. What makes planned giving labor-intensive is that you must continue to steward your donors for the rest of their lives. (How to steward is covered in chapter 7.) What this means is that you have to stay in touch with—talk to and listen to— a donor for 10, 20, 30, or even 50 years.

Major donor fundraising

This approach is the art and science of building relationships and looking after your donors to the point where they naturally want to make a difference by increasing the level of their donation.

The definition of a major gift varies by organization. One of my colleagues went from a grassroots organization where $1,000 was considered a coup to a major medical center. She couldn't believe it when her supervisor told her that she couldn't spend a lot of time with smaller donors, say in the $25,000 range.

The secret to major donor fundraising is to have a small enough cohort of potential donors in order to build relationships. Some experts say that more than 40 donors is not manageable. Many major donor fundraisers, however, have a portfolio of 100 or more. In a small shop, the staff might be expected to do major donor work, send direct mail, host trivia contests, etc. This is why the smaller the organization, the more important board participation becomes. Regardless of an organization's size, board members need training on how to ask and what information to share. You need to set them up for success.

Cause-related marketing

This type of marketing means that a portion of a product sale goes to a charity. The queens of this method of fundraising are the folks at Susan G. Komen. In October, National Breast Cancer Awareness Month, when you open a carton of eggs, some chickens have somehow been taught to lay eggs with a pink ribbon. (When I asked my young grandsons how the chickens could do this, they were as mystified as I was.) The range of corporations that participate, from the NFL and Target to Holland American cruises, is staggering. Will this work for your charity? Yes, *if*:

- You have major corporate contacts.
- Your cause is relatable to most people. (Almost everyone knows someone who has been affected by breast cancer.)
- You have the staff to manage the corporate relationships.

A cosmetic company produced a product where a portion of the sales went to a well-known charity. The nonprofit was shocked when the donor company expected staff at various openings and events explaining the partnership. The nonprofit made about $32,000, but they spent almost $47,000 in staff time, transportation, and expenses. Be careful of what corporations expect from your organization, and be clear who pays for what. At the end of the day, the marketing staff thought it was worth it. The CFO and many board members were less enthusiastic about the return on investment from the partnership.

Crowdfunding

According to Wikipedia, crowdfunding is the practice of funding a project or venture by raising monetary contributions online. It's also a form of crowdsourcing and of alternative finance. In 2015, organizations worldwide raised more than $34 billion in this manner.

By the time you read this book, it could be far higher or, if there is a highly visible case of fraud, much lower.

Crowdfunding will work for you *if*:
- You have a board, volunteer base, or staff that has thousands of email addresses. Email lists can also be purchased.
- You ask to fill a specific need rather than administrative or general support.
- You can stress the urgency for donations.
- You are not looking for sustainable funding but rather project-based financial support.

Summary

Ultimately, planned giving is a cost-effective way to raise funds. But don't forget that planned giving can and should piggyback onto your other forms of fundraising. It might be featured at your special event or included in your direct mail, capital campaign, digital platform, or other fundraising methodologies. If you don't ask, you don't get.

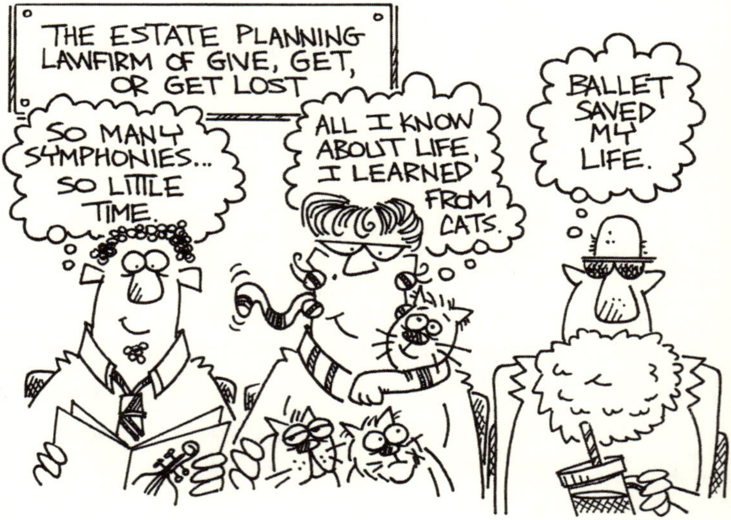

EVERYONE CARES ABOUT SOMETHING DIFFERENT

2

Why do people make planned gifts

Giving has its roots in every organized religion. Mormons tithe 10%. The Koran ordains *zakat*—giving of alms for the poor—for all Muslims who own property or have jobs. The Torah dictates that those of the Jewish faith should pay what might be described as a moral tariff called *tzadakah*. At every Mass, Catholics are expected to put money in a collection plate that is passed from pew to pew. People of faith are used to giving during their lifetimes. Most religions ask once a week. Many charities are afraid to ask more than twice a year. Of course, most charities can't offer a blissful afterlife.

Religious philanthropy is usually focused on helping people who have less than the donor. I personally have a problem with this philosophy. Clean air, a great zoo, or a cure for cancer benefits each and every one of us, regardless of income. In fact, the word "philanthropy," which comes from the Greek *philanthropia*, means love towards mankind. My interpretation is *all* mankind, not just the poor. I believe that we are all beneficiaries of others' charity. As Blanche Dubois memorably said in Tennessee Williams' play *A Streetcar Named Desire*, "I have always depended on the kindness of strangers."

So what are the greatest concerns of a potential donor that need to be resolved before considering a planned gift?

First, will there be enough money for me to live the way I want for the rest of my life? If there is no loved one to shoulder the responsibility for my care, can I afford to remain at home? If my spouse or partner becomes ill, can I afford long-term care? Some people are committed to aging in place and would prefer to stay in their homes to the end of their days. This might mean around-the-clock nursing care, which can be expensive. Others prefer the sociability, ease, and convenience of a senior living community.

Sometimes the perception of available funds has nothing to do with reality. Consider the case of two friends. Joan and Gracie were best friends in prep school. Both had advanced degrees from prestigious universities. Both married and had two children. Both divorced in their early fifties. Joan's husband was an alcoholic. Ten years into the marriage, she became the primary breadwinner. They lived modestly. What she didn't know was that her husband had a problem not only with alcohol but also with Internet gambling.

When all their funds were depleted, including an inheritance from her mother that had not been commingled, and when his profligate spending and the theft of his wife's inheritance were exposed, he committed suicide. Gracie's life was quite different. Married to a prominent surgeon, she was able to dedicate herself to volunteering and raising her family. When her husband was 52, he had an affair with a nurse. A pregnancy resulted, and he divorced Gracie.

Fast forward to both women age 65. Joan and Gracie were living on about the same amount of money. Joan had paid off her husband's gambling debts, was continuing to work and had enough money for Pilates, Starbucks and an occasional trip to the West Coast to visit her daughter and son. She was happy with her life. Gracie, on the other hand, had to go to work for the first time in her mid-fifties. Her fellow sales staff at Saks Fifth Avenue cursed her wayward husband. Her shopping was limited to Target, and she felt bereft, angry, and impoverished. When they looked to the future, Joan was filled with optimism. She started a new consulting venture and, encouraged by her children, signed up for the eHarmony dating site. When Gracie turned 65, she contemplated both suicide and homicide. Neither of her children called. They had chosen team Daddy. Joan felt confident she would have a stable and secure future and when she wrote her will, left 10% to charity. Gracie didn't have a will. She often read Gothic novels of the 20th century and called herself "a distressed gentlewoman," a phrase she said to herself in the mirror with downcast eyes.

Same background, same education, same marital themes of betrayal and divorce, yet a totally different perception of their ability to provide for themselves.

One of the issues you might need to explore when approaching a potential donor is whether they believe they have enough to live on for the rest of their lives. Some forms of giving result in a monthly annuity, providing the donor an income that can ease financial anxieties. Again, asking the right question will determine if this concern is realistic.

Financial advisors can be helpful in these situations. One advisor I know had a client whose wife was so insecure about money that she tried to block every charitable gift her husband wanted to give. It came to a head in the wealth manager's office. The wife said, "What happens if you are gone and I need medical care?" The husband replied, "There is enough money for you to build a damn hospital!" She looked at the advisor, who said, "Well, at least a very large wing." They all laughed and began to discuss the reality of the wealth available. The wife came to understand that her husband's desire to give away some of *their* loot would not diminish the quality of *her* life.

The biggest challenge for parents is determining the amount of money to leave their children as well as the logistics. What is fair? What is too much? When should the heirs receive the funds? Should they get a lump sum or a trust over a span of 10, 20, or 30 years? When they reach a certain age, or when they reach certain landmarks such as college graduation or marriage? How do you divide your estate when you have one child living in a home for developmentally disabled adults, one running a hedge fund with a taste for bachelor toys like high-performance sports cars, and the youngest married, with four children, to a kind man who works in a hardware store? She happily teaches grade school, grows her own veggies, and is active in their church, which is a little too way out for the parents. This is just the tip of the parental challenges.

Consider the challenges of this couple: The woman married her second husband in her early 60s. She never wanted children, so had none. Her husband had two, one in high school and one just out of college. Even though the husband had been divorced from his first wife for more than a decade, the kids hoped that their parents would reconcile and detested their stepmother. The husband had been a reporter, but, as newspaper staffs shrank, he was laid off. His freelance work brought in nowhere near his previous salary and offered no benefits. Two years into their marriage, the wife received an inheritance. It was estate planning time. Her mouth dropped open when her husband asked, "How are you going to take care of my children?"

That was two years ago. They haven't gotten past it. The charity the wife wants to leave her estate to is champing at the bit. The husband is hurt. The children are angry. They believe Dad's new wife should pay off the college loans for the oldest and shell out tuition for the youngest—ideas fueled by their mother, wife No. 1. The wise gift officer suggested the couple consider counseling to resolve this issue, as the most important thing was to have a happy marriage. I am not sure he truly felt this way, but he knew his charity wasn't going to see a dime if this situation wasn't resolved, and, while relatively young, the wife smoked three packs a day of unfiltered Camels. To date there is no progress, but marital counseling is on the table.

So, how much to leave your children? Not just millionaires grapple with this issue. Jennifer Wooldridge is the CEO of a nonprofit that cares for people with developmental and other disabilities. Her mother was a 17-year old German woman who married her dad,

SOME CHILDREN PERCEIVE
PLANNED GIVING
AS THE ENEMY
OF INHERITANCE.

a GI stationed in Bad Kreuznach, West Germany. Jennifer had a middle-class upbringing and lived all over the world as an "Army brat." When she was 27, she married Joe, a meat cutter. They had two children and now have four grandchildren. As they look toward the future, their philosophy is that children and grandchildren should be self-sufficient and not rely on inheritances or financial gifts.

That said, she also wants them to learn to be givers to those who have less. She believes that our purpose as human beings is to do the best we can to make other peoples' lives better. If something is left over at the time of their deaths, Jennifer and Joe want their children to remain self-sufficient, and with any money they might receive, enjoy some and give some away. The couple's estate plan calls for their son to take care of the estate, which includes a planned gift to the nonprofit Jennifer works for. After the charitable gift, their daughter gets 50% and her son gets the other 50%. Her children know her values, and they know that she would want them to share with others.

Joe has five siblings, one of whom is disabled. The parent's estate is focused on making life the best possible for their disabled son. If he predeceases his five siblings, however, the remainder goes to the five. Joe and his siblings all back this plan, which makes them an extraordinary family.

Jennifer's husband Joe believes that estate planning should not be a one-time occurrence but rather a task reviewed every few years. She is a follower of the American psychologist Abraham Maslow and has told her children that basic needs such as housing come before toys. Her philosophy: Take care of your needs first, then a charity's, then and only then, take care of your desires. Jennifer's father is still alive, and if there is a small inheritance she plans to purchase a bench in his honor at the national cemetery Jefferson Barracks, where her mother is buried.

Why do people give in their lifetime?

Some folks give because they enjoy recognition. I feel they sometimes get a bad rap as being egotistical. As the beneficiary of the generosity of others, I like to know who gave the money. It inspires and warms me. I take tap dancing classes at a nonprofit called Center of Creative Arts. When I walk down the hall, I see the name of my mother's friend Lucy Lopata on the office she donated. The studio I dance in was donated by Meyer Kranzberg. I met his daughter-in-law Nancy. How can you not like someone who bursts into the song "Red Headed Woman" when you first meet her? (Especially since I pay a lot to be a redhead.) Because of the Kranzberg's generosity, if AARP revives *A Chorus Line*, I will be ready to audition. When I take my grandchildren to the zoo, I always point out the names of generous patrons who wanted children like my grandkids to see puffins and tigers. We talk about the risk of extinction, the fragility of nature, and the breeding program that will hopefully stop or slow the extinction.

For our children's birthdays, in addition to a party, a present, and a cake, we make a donation to the charity of their choice. The specifics of how and when to do this are outlined in my previous book *Raising Charitable Children*. When our son Jono was six, he chose Craft Alliance Gallery, a nonprofit that comprises both exhibition space and classrooms. He started taking clay classes at Craft Alliance when he was four. He chose it because he feared they might run out of clay. Now, decades later, he is a ceramics teacher. When he takes his students to exhibits at Craft Alliance, he always shows them the brick in front of the building that bears his name. Furthermore, Jono was given the honor of being proclaimed the first donor to the Gallery's 1985 capital campaign. We gave on his behalf because we wanted him to know that there was more in this world for him to think about than the long list of things he coveted.

So why do people make plans to be generous *after* their passing?

According to planned giving guru Dr. Russell James of Texas Tech University, planned giving can do two things:
- Lower taxes
- Trade a gift for income

I don't disagree with his premise, but I think it is more complicated.

Here are a few more reasons to make planned gifts:

- You want to help an organization that helped you... when your house was ravaged by a forest fires, you received food, kindness, and sanctuary. You lost all your belongings, but thanks to this nonprofit, you didn't lose your dignity. You want to honor their assistance at a low point in your life.
- You want to feel needed...you found a way to help children after your kids grew up, and you want the program and your involvement to continue.
- You want to act out a fantasy...you always wanted to be a ballet dancer but didn't have the money to take lessons. You want to support another child's dreams to wear a pink tutu and glide across a stage.
- You want to right a wrong...you believe your family came down on the wrong side of a civil rights issue, so you want to support an organization that supports the rights of those your family scorned. I know a woman from the South who put the NAACP in her will after her grandparents passed away and she found a Klan outfit in their attic.
- You received services and want to make sure others receive them in the future...you had life-saving heart surgery and want it available to future patients. Or better still, a non-surgical cure for heart defects.
- You enjoy recognition...you worked hard for every dollar you earned and want to set an example that others can rise from poverty and give generously.

- You want to feel needed...you found a way to help children after your kids grew up, and you want the program and your involvement to continue.
- You have children...your daughter recovered in a drug treatment center you'd like to thank. Or perhaps your son continues to use drugs after multiple interventions and rehab programs, and you would rather give your estate to a cause you love rather than to fuel his addiction.
- You believe in the need for a safety net...you have relatives who were helped by Catholic Charities, Lutheran Family and Children Services, or Jewish Family and Children's Services and want others to find help if they need it.
- You want to honor a family member...your mother was the first woman pilot in your state and you want to set up a scholarship in her name.
- You find it therapeutic...you came from an abusive home and want other children to get the help you never received.
- You are religious... your place of worship is dear to you. But it is also very old, and you want it to thrive. You also want the roof, plumbing, and electrical systems to work.
- You have a family tradition of planned giving...your grandparents left money to the Humane Society; your parents, also animal lovers, left money to the Humane Society; and your new puppy, Scruffy,

adopted from the Humane Society, believes you should give. You give despite the meal Scruffy made of your brand new, very expensive shoes.
- You feel there is no one else to do it...your family is afflicted with a rare genetic disease you want cured. You give now, and, if there is not a cure in your lifetime, you want to give after your passing so that other families don't suffer as well.
- You want to have a significant impact...you only had so much money in your lifetime, but with the aid of a life insurance policy, you can ensure that your favorite nonprofit can expand its reach.
- You work for a nonprofit... you love the cause and believe that you should make a planned gift before you ask someone else for one.
- You want to advocate for equality...your mother told you when you were a child that the world is unfair, but you want to continue to support organizations that are devoted to leveling the playing field.
- You want to gain status...you want a pin to wear among people you respect that says you are a legacy giver to an organization you value.
- You give because you were asked...this is my case. Although I've worked as a consultant to nonprofits since 1994, the Girl Scouts were the first group that asked me directly for a planned gift.
- You give because of who asked...I gave to the Girl Scouts because Dianne Belk asked me, and she is someone I respect.

- You want to be an agent of change...you stopped saying long ago that someone should do something and discovered an organization devoted to the change you believe in. You got involved, and you want that involvement to last.
- You want to bring people joy...you remember your first visit to the symphony in the days of Leonard Bernstein and want your children and grandchildren to feel a similar rapture.
- You feel guilty...when your mother was dying, you couldn't or wouldn't leave your work, life, and family to travel halfway across the country to be with her, but hospice took good care of her. You want to honor their caring and shed some guilt.
- You want to be a watchdog...you are pro-choice or pro-life and you want an organization that shares your point of view to prevail.

When potential donors have incorrect information:

Grassroots fundraising consultant Kim Klein shared a story about her mother, Phyllis Klein, who died in 2016 at the age of 89. Phyllis had joined the YWCA in Boulder, Colorado, in the early 1950s, giving her the distinction of being its oldest member. She loved the YWCA and embraced its mission to end racism and empower women. The executive director (ED) often chatted with Phyllis and became a friend. When Phyllis was in her early 80s, the ED said to her:

"We're thinking of ratcheting up our legacy giving efforts but need to think through how to do that. We want to talk with people about leaving us money in their wills or estate plans but aren't quite sure how to do that respectfully. We are seeking advice from long-time members like yourself. How would you feel if we asked you to leave us a gift in your will?"

"Well, I know that I am going to die," said Phyllis, "so I'd feel fine about it. But I know that I can't make a planned gift because you have to leave a minimum of $10,000 and I can't do that."

"Actually, that's not true," the ED explained. "You can leave a dollar or stock or jewelry, or almost anything."

Kim's mother was puzzled by this information, so she asked several friends about it. Many of them also thought $10,000 was the minimum. Who knows how this misinformation had seeped into the Boulder water, but the ED assured Phyllis this was not the case. She then arranged for a gift in her estate to the YWCA and encouraged others to do the same. When people don't give when we ask, we often take it personally. A more mature approach considers that something else entirely may be going on—in this case, widespread misinformation.

One last point. Spending money on a will is an excellent investment. As of this writing, in the state of Missouri, if you die without a will and have an estate worth more than $1 million, the state will assign an attorney and the estate will be billed no less than $26,000. You don't have to be a control freak to realize that investing in a will can save those you love thousands of your hard-earned dollars. And if your children are minors, the state will make decisions for them.

Summary

Just as you have a wide range of stories to share about how your nonprofit makes a difference, your donors have their own stories. As a nonprofit leader, your job is to find out why your donors care, so that you can help them with ways to make a legacy of their caring and passion. And yes, Dr. James is correct: By giving a planned gift, you can receive income during your life *and* save on taxes.

Choosing the right person to do the ask will make the difference between receiving a planned gift and your donor wanting to shower after the meeting.

3

Who to ask

Start with your Board

If those legally, morally, and fiscally responsible for your mission don't believe enough in your charity to make a planned gift, it is a waste of time asking others. According to BoardSource, 62% of *board members* are 50 and over, which means that they are in the core demographic for planned giving.

After explaining why planned giving is a useful tool for fundraising, sustainability, endowment, and the future of the organization, you might want to do a simple survey, perhaps at a board retreat. Here is a sample survey, which I believe should be done anonymously:

Do you have an estate plan? ___yes___no

If yes, do you have charitable gifts in your plan?
___yes___no

If yes, have you included our organization?
___yes___no.

If no, would you consider a gift to our organization?
___yes___no

OPTIONAL: Would you be willing to share your name? _____

I did this exercise with the board of a local Ohio chapter of a large international nonprofit. It turned out that eight of the 23 board members had a planned gift to this charity in their estate plans. Six chose to share their names. The executive director was so excited I thought she was going to jump over the table and kiss me. She had no idea. I asked the group what this survey told them. Here are their responses:

- We have a board that is truly committed.
- We have a brand that we trust.
- I really must get an estate plan, but what with this season of *Dancing with the Stars* and *Monday Night Football*, plus the expense, I just haven't gotten it together. Other board members chimed in, "If not now, when? Will you at least make an appointment to get it done by the next meeting?" The people without estate plans said yes.
- One board member confessed that making a will means acknowledging that she is going to die. The oldest board member, at 86, reassured her that she was going to die and that having a will was why he had lived so long. She later shared that, based on his wisdom, she made an appointment the next day and included the charity in her will. She made the gift in his honor.

- The board members who had an estate plan did not stress the obligation to give to the charity but rather the need to protect one's family. They talked about probate with the same degree of foreboding one talks about getting HIV or Ebola. Probate, they stressed, is something you want to avoid.
- Some said that they would gladly be interviewed for the nonprofit's website to share why they had made a planned gift. Others felt their donation was private and did not want public recognition.
- A few mused that if the organization has this many people committed without asking, what would happen if we did ask?
- Some revealed how they orchestrated the gift. One said that 10% of his estate goes to charity, the rest to relatives. The charities are listed by percentage, the highest percentage going to boards of organizations on which he has served.

The discussion continued throughout dinner. The board was excited about protecting their future, their family's future, and building on the gifts of time and money they had already invested in a nonprofit they loved.

Follow up

- The ED and board chair graciously thanked all those who had shared that they had made a planned gift, reaffirmed the promise of privacy for board members who did not want to be publicly acknowledged and asked who would publicly discuss why they gave. Some said they would be glad to speak about it at the annual meeting; some said they were willing to be videotaped; and some said they would be willing to be acknowledged in the annual report.

- The board members decided to contact their national office to learn more about rolling out a planned giving campaign, as well as to ask for copies of legal documents and policies.
- This board retreat was eight years ago. The ED reported that all her board members had created estate plans and more than 68% had included a planned gift to the charity. While 100% annual giving should be expected of all board members, 60% legacy donors should be considered a home run. (I have colleagues who believe it should be 100%, but some people don't believe in giving to charity after their death. As one such person said to me, "I have given to my place of worship my entire life. I have given to the United Way my entire working career. I have given to the favorite causes of my friends, relatives, and clients, and sometimes their children. Enough is enough. I have four children and nine grandchildren. It's their turn." I respect this point of view.
- The final thing the staff did at the end of every call was to ask how the donor wanted to be acknowledged. This is not something you should assume or guess. Make sure you get it right. Here are a few possibilities:

- Carol Weisman & Frank Robbins, MD
- Dr. Patricia Wolff and Judge Michael Wolff
- The Londoff Family
- The Beggs-Griesedieck Family Foundation
- The Wanda Wood Donor Advised Fund

The bottom line is that you need to ask donors if they want to be acknowledged and, if so, how. Skip this step at your peril!

Also, giving in one's lifetime has certain perks such as a little bit of flattery and some interesting invitations. It is also better to give in your lifetime if you have enough funds to live on because there are tax benefits that bequests do not have.

Using this technique with another board I worked with resulted in a very different scenario. There were 15 members, 14 of whom had estate plans. Not one included this charity in their plan. When polled, nine board members said they would consider it. Pretty interesting results. John, the board chair and a lawyer, said that he would champion this effort. I told him he had to make his own planned gift before soliciting others so that he could say, "Will you join me as a legacy donor?" John said he would get it done within 48 hours. He looked at the board and said, "This survey was anonymous, so I am planning to get together with all of you." His area of law was not estate planning, and he was going to have a partner in his firm do it, so he wasn't bucking for business. He was, however, serious about getting the board on the planned giving bandwagon.

Another tale from the boardroom

Sometimes, as a nonprofit leader, you will inspire folks to make a planned gift. But, sometimes, it is you who will be inspired by the creativity of your donors in the way they give. Here is an example.

During dinner after a nonprofit retreat, a board member shared his philosophy of giving. He was a widower in his 80s. I'll call him Sam. His words are imprinted on my brain. Our conversation went something like this:

Carol: Do you mind me asking if you have gifts to nonprofits in your estate?

Sam: Not at all. I have six children, and I decided to divide my estate by seven. The seventh portion is for a child or children who do not have someone to care about them or love them.

Carol: How did you set it up?

Sam: All six kids must agree on how to distribute the seventh portion. They don't always agree on things. In fact, they usually don't agree on things.

Carol: Imagine that!

Sam: I think one of my daughters-in-law might even be a Democrat!

Carol: Oh my!

Sam: The seventh child will be getting in the "healthy seven or eight figures," so the kids can divvy up the money any number of ways. They can give it to one child or several, to one specific organization or to numerous nonprofits. They just have to agree. Until they decide how to spend the money for the seventh child, no one gets a dime.

Carol: You sound like a bit of a control freak, but one who covers your bases. I admire that.

Sam, laughing: I admit it. I am a total control junkie. Yelling at my children when they were only two was clearly a losing game. By their teen years, I was unbelievably adrift. It turns out you can't fire your kids. Thank the Lord for my sensible and understanding wife.

Carol: How did you come up with the concept of the seventh child?

Sam: I decided that after my death I wanted three things for my children. I wanted them to agree on something. I wanted them to have a meaningful conversation about philanthropy, to know that they were responsible for more than their own happiness. And I wanted them to remember that I'd been a seventh child who'd grown up in an orphanage. Without the kindness and generosity of others, who gave me friendship, scholarships, advice and a helping hand, there would be no money to divide.

His face took on an odd expression.

Carol: You look sad.

Sam: We had so little in the orphanage, and yet we shared. I gave my children so much, and yet I failed to teach them the basic concept of taking care of one another. I am afraid I pitted them against one another and we are all suffering from my idiotic approach to parenting. Their mother tried her best to persuade me to be less harsh, but I didn't listen. It is my one true regret. I have even done a video apologizing for my poor parenting. Damn it, it's not over until it's over. It's an important lesson no matter when they learn it.

With that, he went outside to smoke a cigar.

When I told this story to estate-planning attorney Larry Katzenstein, he said that it was an interesting case and he wondered if Sam's children understood that if they gave the money to a nonprofit, the tax consequences would be quite different than if they gave it outright to a single child. "The children need a smart estate planning expert involved in the process," said Larry. "Sam's children might not care about the tax implications, but it could make all the difference in the world whether a charity or the government received the lion's share."

When we talk to our donors about planned giving, consider asking them what they want to leave their children besides money. I think Sam had it right. It's not over til it's over.

Asking staff

I facilitated a retreat with a medium-sized nonprofit. I had a private session with five of their development staff members. All were under 30, three married, two with children, one engaged, one single. Not one had a will. What are the barriers to young people having wills? The first answer that came up when I queried this small sample of nonprofit employees: Money. One said that if he had enough money to have a will written, say $300, he would rather take a camping trip for 10 days. Others chimed in with how they would spend the $300. One of the young women said that she had spent her disposable income whittling down her $147,000 in student loans to under $100,000.

When asking front line staff, such as caregivers at residential facilities, the answer to why they didn't have an estate plan was the same as that for the under-thirties: Money. Some said that if they had enough money to pay for a will, they would rather buy new track shoes for some grandchild or Easter clothes for the whole family. There was also the assumption that they did not have anything to leave. I reminded one woman that she had a life insurance policy through work. She jerked her head up and said that her no-good-rotten-ex-husband was the recipient of the policy and that she needed to make an immediate change. A male coworker suggested that she make him the new beneficiary; another suggested the nonprofit. Unfortunately, and all too common, she didn't have her affairs in order. Divorce is traumatic and not every "i" is dotted and every "t" crossed when a marriage ends.

Lawyers typically charge a flat fee to write a will and other basic estate planning documents. The low end for a simple lawyer-drafted will is around $300. A cost closer to $1,000 is more common, and it's not unusual to find a $1,200+ price tag. I have a mentor who paid $50,000 for his estate plan. His wife said, "This is ridiculous. You can't control our lives after your death. Unless you miss the old New York phone books, do something simpler," which he did. When you have a blended family, children with special needs, property in different states, minor children in different states or countries, and the list goes on, then you are not talking about a simple will, and the charges will reflect that complexity.

There are several ways to help your staff ensure the safety of their families' assets as well as consider a charitable donation

You might ask a board member for a restricted gift per employee for the going minimum rate in your community toward a will for every staff person. You could offer a list of attorneys who would accept this fee. If the estate plan costs more, the employee would be responsible for the difference. You will need to educate staff on the options they have and the decisions they will need to make.

I believe that, especially in residential care facilities, if your staff members have wills, your clients will too, because they talk to one another. Many of the staff work long hours for low wages because they genuinely care about the people they serve. They want them well taken care of. A typical scenario, which drives many of my clients nuts, is that the facility cares for a person for 10-15 years, and then when the patient becomes terminally ill hospice comes in, does a fabulous job, and the family requests that donations go to hospice.

This almost happened in our family. My mother-in-law was in a wonderful continuous care retirement community for years. When she reached the end of treatment for her cancer, she had a hospice team that was first-class. My brother-in-law wanted donations to go to hospice. I reminded him that the place where she had lived provided great care for more than 15 years. He reminded me of an episode six years before her death that was troublesome. My view was that everyone periodically slips. We ultimately decided to give more money to the facility that had been her bedrock for so many years. We recognized the excellent hospice care but in a smaller way.

I believe that if you are operating a 24-hour facility and take care of your staff and their families, your turnover will be lower and your planned giving higher. I am currently working with a consortium of continuous care communities and a law firm. We are going to see if my supposition is correct. The employees will be offered this benefit in eight of the 17 residential care centers. We will track the planned giving by residents and their families in the years to come. I hope to report the findings in the next edition of this book and on my blog.

An important caveat: There should be no pressure to give a gift to your organization. In the past, nonprofits put great pressure on employees to give, which created resentment. (This was and continues to be an issue in communities of faith as well as in payroll deduction programs.) You want a gift that touches the heart, not wrenches the gut and squeezes the wallet.

One client hated to go to church because of the pressure to give in every sermon. Finally, he had it out with the priest. The priest said, "All money belongs to God." His congregant said, "But you aren't God" and changed churches.

I know a gentleman who was told that he would find out about his raise after he'd filled out his donation card for the local United Way. His boss was chairing the campaign that year. The employee's favorite charity was not a recipient of funds from the federated group, which collects for many nonprofits by using payroll deductions and then doling out the funds using various criteria. He gave, reluctantly, and got the raise. He gave to his favorite charity from his home account. Twenty-seven years later, after the employee left this corporation, the federated giving program asked him for a planned gift. He said no.

Asking volunteers

For decades, I have attended Toastmasters with Alan Raymond, a retired accountant and avid gardener. He huffed in one day and said to me, "You won't believe what happened. I am a master gardener and I volunteer for a park and they actually wrote me a letter asking for money. You wouldn't believe how much time I spend there."

He was clearly agitated.

"Do you give to other charities?" I asked him.

"Of course."

He started to list them.

I asked him, "Do you know this nonprofit better than the other ones you give to, some of which are half way around the world?"

"Well, yes."

"So, you know what they need and whether funds are spent wisely?"

"Well, yes."

"Then why not build on the time you give and invest money where you spend your time?"

"I never thought of it that way."

The conversation ended with Alan saying he'd consider giving to the park where he volunteered so much of his time.

I think I know what happened. Someone wrote him a lousy letter, which did not acknowledge the importance and value of his contribution as a volunteer master gardener. Instead of feeling like a valued volunteer, he felt like an ATM. Worse, he felt as if the organization valued his money more than his time and skills. He had never received a thank you for all of his back-breaking work that contributed to the bottom line.

Should volunteers be asked for money? It is worth noting that this question doesn't come up when we solicit money from board members, even though they are also volunteers who give time all year long. A hundred years ago, the major difference between a board member and other volunteers was gender. Now some folks seem to hold the stereotype that board members are wealthy, while frontline volunteers are poor. Both are faulty assumptions. It's usually paid staff who push back at the thought of asking volunteers to donate. "They shouldn't be asked. They give their time."

The mindset should be the opposite. Volunteers are in the trenches. They've demonstrated in person their commitment to your mission. You can feel safe in assuming these people care a lot and understand how much more is needed. Note, too, that with many nonprofits moving toward term limits for board members, your corps of hands-on volunteers are the people who can stay with you for decades, and perhaps already have.

To give you an idea of the scope of opportunity of working with volunteers, Independent Sector reported in 2016 that 63 million Americans volunteered about eight billion hours, worth $193 billion of time. This cohort of your inner circle should not be ignored.

Give your volunteers the opportunity to embrace your organization in an additional way. It is not up to either board or staff members to make a financial decision for another person. Here are just a few of the reasons to ask them:
- Volunteers know what your organization needs, whether it is a coffee machine in the waiting room, a new wheelbarrow, or a larger building.
- They have stories about why they volunteer and how the mission is important to them. Have volun-

teers ask volunteers. Peer to peer always has power. Let them tell their stories in your other fundraising initiatives.

- Volunteers can explain the details of how the organizational mission is accomplished.
- A study released by Fidelity Charitable Gift Fund and Volunteer Match reports that 67% of Americans who volunteered in the past year say they "generally make their financial donations to the same organizations where they volunteer."
- Volunteers donate, on average, 10 times more than non-volunteers.
- Marketing is easy since your potential donors are usually on the premises. On the other hand, if your organization relies on volunteers who do their work in the field (troop leaders, sports coaches, friendly visitors) or, increasingly, online, it's easy for them to become invisible. When you ask for any kind of financial donation, especially a planned gift, remote volunteers need more personal outreach.
- Three ways to guarantee your volunteers consider becoming major or planned givers:
  • Thank them for their volunteer work.
  • Listen to them.
  • Ask them to give money as well as time.

If you are telling your story in written form through appeal letters, annual reports, mission statements, or newsletters, consider my favorite source for anything written: guru Tom Ahern. Get his books. Listen to his YouTube videos and webinars. Believe me, if you use his methods, your volunteers will feel honored, appreciated, and generous.

The value of the work of volunteers cannot be underestimated. Many of these folks can make a capital campaign or a major gift. All should be asked for a planned gift. It is up to them to say yes or no.

The Queen of Volunteerism and keeper of secrets to successful volunteer management is Susan Ellis. To get the most out of your volunteers and for them to get the most out of working with you, take a deep dive into her website, www.EnergizeInc.com.

One more suggestion: Don't assume that a volunteer is not already a donor. Many organizations don't compare their volunteer list to their donor list. It is like assuming a blonde can't also be smart! (I have been blonde and used it as an excuse for lack of knowledge. It didn't work.) Also, you need to check the addresses of your donors and your volunteers. A check might have the husband's name first and the wife's name second, and she might be the volunteer, or it could be a teenager or adult child living at home. The kiss of death is sending the same family multiple appeals without realizing that they live in the same household. A frequent scenario in our home is when my husband gets a thank-you note for a gift I sent. I only get mildly aggravated, but a misaddressed acknowledgement is not motivating. You can always call or email if you aren't sure who is the donor, however I always send a card with my name on it with the check. The good news is that Frank is usually very pleased when he learns that we have donated to a cause we've discussed.

Who is the ideal donor?

An ideal donor for a capital campaign is a person, couple, corporation or foundation with both an interest in your mission and immediate capacity. Immediate capacity might mean a check today or a series of payments—usually three to five— over many years. An ideal donor for a planned gift has some of these qualities but might not have immediate capacity. Who you are looking for:

- Someone who has been giving any amount for 10 years or more.
- Someone who is childless. This trait is the biggest indicator for a planned gift. If someone is not only a parent but also a grandparent, the chances of a planned gift drop from 10% to 5%. My belief is that if parents believe they have raised great kids, they want to support them, and if they believe their children turned out poorly, they hope the issues skip a generation. Dr. Paul Schervish, who is one of the great nonprofit researchers, shared this story at a conference: "I told my son that he was a better father than I was. My son said, "Thank you, Dad, but why

do you say that?" Dr. Schervish replied, "Because your children turned out better than mine."
- Someone who has the capacity to give a gift. (Frankly, this is almost anyone, but time is limited, so you want to start with folks with the greatest capacity.)
- Someone who has volunteered for your organization.
- Someone who says, "I wish I could do more." That is the phrase that pays.
- People in their 50s and 60s. In 2016, 68% of people over 65 and 56% of people between 50 and 64 had wills. (Gallup, 2016)
- In my own experience, and this is only anecdotal, I have found that few people change their wills after their mid-80s. When I talked to estate planning expert Larry Katzenstein, he had a different opinion. A gentleman who was 88 had just come into Larry's office to update his estate plan, which he had drafted 60 years earlier. Obviously, there are differing opinions on this subject, but I was unable to find statistical data.

Who might *not* be the first person to approach for a planned gift?

One of the eyeball-roll-inducing comments often heard in a boardroom is why not ask...fill in the regional philanthropist's name. For instance, Oprah Winfrey's name was always mentioned when she lived in Chicago; Tyler Perry's name comes up in Atlanta; Steven Spielberg, George Lucas and a zillion other generous

Hollywood luminaries are mentioned in Los Angeles. When one of the usual suspects is named, the next questions you need to ask are:
- Has this person ever given to our charity before?
- Does anyone in the room know this person?
- Does s(he) know about our organization?
- Does s(he) have a history of being interested in the work we do?
- If so, is s(he) already committed to another organization?
- What is our strategy to get him or her interested? Get a phone number? Get an email address?
- Does anyone know how to get past the myriad gatekeepers, or better still, does anyone in our organization know the gatekeepers?

The answers range from:
- She really should care.
- I once read in *People* magazine that he had a friend who died of the disease we are trying to cure.
- I had a hairstylist whose sister was his wife's manicurist, but she left town 12 years ago.

Only once in the past 24 years have I worked with a board with multiple points of access to a billionaire. I asked the executive committee, "What about Mr. Billionaire? Is there a possibility we could cultivate him?" One board member said, "Well, I don't know him that well, but we play golf at least once a year." A second committee member said, "We've had Thanksgiving together for the past 10 years, but rarely meet the rest of the year." A third board member said, "We went to grad school together and were quite close then."

I was speechless—a rare event, as anyone who knows me can attest.

I asked if any of these men had Mr. Billionaire's personal phone number. They all said they did. I couldn't believe it. What I didn't realize at the time was how intimidated they all were by the Billionaire. Though all three board members were über-rich, they did not see him as a peer. Each man wanted someone else to call, but finally they agreed on a plan. They would try to get an appointment when two of the three could meet with him. It took 18 months to schedule. (Don't be discouraged when it takes more than a day or two to schedule a talk with a major prospect.) They had hoped for an initial gift of $10 million. They got $100,000. How many of you would be happy with an *initial* gift of six figures? Had Mr. Billionaire been stewarded, more money would have come.

The rest is a sad story. The three board members assured everyone that the gift of $100,000 was a "get lost" gift. Their capital campaign consultant and I insisted that because this nonprofit was new, a $100,000 initial gift was not necessarily a brush off but rather a nibble before an ultimate banquet of giving. The board ignored us and never again contacted Mr. Billionaire for another gift.

Lessons learned:
- When you have access, don't expect a gigantic gift off the bat. It could happen, but it rarely does.
- It can take a long time to get on someone's schedule when you are dealing with extremely busy people who travel, own several homes, or are in court or an operating room for large blocks of time. I had one exasperated administrative assistant tell me that she believed the Normandy Invasion might not have been as difficult to plan.
- Send the person who knows the potential planned donor the best or who would have the best rapport.
- Have a stewardship plan in mind for the next gift, and the next, and the next, and ultimately a planned gift.
- These folks knew the donor. They knew how to steward him, what he would have liked, what could have touched him. They didn't steward him because they considered $100,000 a "get lost" gift. They assumed a disinterest on his part.
- No one followed up.
- This is a tragedy that never reached the final act. Act I: Get the appointment. Act II (which they skipped): Cultivate the relationship. Act III: Make the ask. Act IV (which never happened): Graciously say thank you and provide an update on how the funds were used and the impact of the gift. The big bucks come in the fourth act. Without Acts II and IV, this drama played out as incomplete.

Who to ask next?

After board and staff and volunteers, the next folks to approach are annual and major givers.

I am on a board where the development director asked me what level of donor I would be willing to call. She suggested $500 and up. I suggested $1 and up. Former Mayor Michael Bloomberg's first gift to Johns Hopkins University was $5. Today, he is the first person in the U.S. to give more than a billion dollars to a university. And he continues to give.

Small, consistent donors have the same challenge many of us do: liquidity, as mentioned before. In the U.S. today, only 10% of a person's assets are liquid. The rest are tied up in real estate, bonds, stocks, insurance, and various financial instruments. Planned giving to an organization they love makes all the sense in the world. It is much easier to get a planned gift from these folks than a capital or endowment fund gift. Also, they are usually not thanked or asked enough and are fun to talk to. You can point out tax incentives and lifetime income benefits.

When acknowledging a donor in an annual report or online, include a section on long-term donors as well as large donors. Send anniversary cards at 5, 10, 15, 20 years thanking them for their ceaseless support. Take them to lunch or dinner. Find a meaningful memento to thank them.

A conversation that I had as a board member with a small, consistent donor went something like this:

Carol: Hello, this is Carol Weisman and I am a board member for XYZ organization. I am calling to follow up on the invitation we sent you to a cocktail party for our valued donors.

Donor: I wish I could give more. I'm not sure you have all the correct information about my giving. I don't have a lot to give. I am available, but are you sure you want me?

Carol: I wish I could give more as well. There are ways to get this done for those of us who don't have a lot of spare cash around. Have you ever thought about remembering our charity in your will?

Donor: Well, I was going to update my will since my sister passed and the entire farm is mine and my kids don't want it. I want to spend the rest of my days here. My husband died 23 years ago. My kids tell me that if I get cranky in my old age, my ashes will go on the compost heap, instead of under my favorite oak tree.

Carol: I hear you. Our son is a ceramicist and made our funeral urns for a Christmas gift when he was in high school. But getting back to our charity, there are ways of giving now, staying on the farm, getting a tax deduction, and receiving recognition for your generosity and dedication to our cause.

Donor: How does that work?

Carol: I've been known to practice medicine without a license, but not law. Would you like me to have one of our planned giving officers call you? Darryl Redhage is the one who helped me. He has made a planned gift to our organization and he is an absolute delight.

Donor: That sounds great.

Carol: What is the best way to get hold of you? Email? Cell phone? Landline? Carrier pigeon?

Donor: I hate email. My phone is still attached to the wall and I like it that way. Have him call me any time after 5 a.m.

Carol: Thank you so much for caring and giving. You are appreciated. If you have any other questions, my landline is 314-863-4422. It is also attached to the wall! By the way, I will be passing your house on the way to the party. Would you like me to pick you up? We can talk about our charity and compare notes on our rascally children.

Donor: Sounds great. 6:00?

Carol: I'll be there.

Follow up is crucial. The staff person needs to be contacted immediately so that (s)he can set up the meeting with the potential donor. If the death of the sister was recent, you might also want to send a condolence letter. As most know in this century, Google is a great tool to confirm the date when the sister died.

When you call longtime donors, whether large or small, the first order of business is to thank them for their loyalty. You probably should not thank them for their generosity unless you know this was, in fact, a generous gift. Ten thousand dollars is chump change to some of your donors and the gift of a lifetime for others. If they say that they are already planned givers, invite them to your reception or event. If possible, meet with them before the event and assess whether this donor or couple should be sharing their story about how they made the decision. You might want to seat them at a specific table so that they can encourage other potential donors.

Summary

Asking for a planned gift is different from asking for an annual, major, or capital gift in that the money comes out of different pockets. For a capital gift, you would go to those with the largest capacity, even if their relationship to the mission and organization is minimal. For a planned gift, you want to consider three demographics when you prioritize your time: those who have a long history of giving, those who have no children, and those with the greatest capacity.

ARE YOU SURE THERE'S NOT
A BETTER WAY
TO DO DONOR RESEARCH?

4

How to research your donors

The more you know about your donor, the better your chances of procuring a gift for your nonprofit that is a joyful experience your donor wants to repeat. Your goal should be nothing short of making a gift to your organization the best philanthropic experience of your donor's life.

One of the most valuable currencies you have is time. You must know how to mine your database to determine where to invest the most effort. Whether you are a board member, staff person, or volunteer, you want to know about people who:
- Care about your cause
- Are generous
- Have the means to make your time worthwhile
- Are already donors
- Have volunteered for your organization
- Attend events

- Are alumni, season-ticket holders, former patients, or other recipients of services

If you don't have a robust and up-to-date database, and if no one in your organization knows your potential donor, Facebook, Google, LinkedIn, and Zillow will be your best resources.

- Facebook will guide you to your donor's passion. Whether you see your donor parasailing, exploring archaeological ruins, or photographed over and over with his dogs, you know what to lead with when you contact him or her. After a deep dive into Facebook, a medical charity development director wrote the potential giver a note on a card that featured a litter of pugs, the donor's obvious passion. The donor called immediately. The development director then set up a meeting, borrowed a dog, and met the potential donor in a dog park. They had an immediate connection and the potential donor became a supporter.
- You never know what you are going to find on Google. You might discover there are 127 Dr. Parks in your city, or you might find out that the Dr. Park you want to speak to is on the PTA of your child's school. Unless you have the name right, Google can feel like sipping from a firehose.
- LinkedIn will give you insight into your potential donor's professional life. Many people have skills you'd never guess. One second-grade teacher had

been a partner at Arthur Andersen. A Ph.D. in neuroanatomy had an undergraduate degree from Cornell in agriculture. A dear friend, Sister Nancy Rose Gucwa, is a cloistered Benedictine nun. She was also in the first class of women at West Point. She isn't on LinkedIn and took a vow of poverty, but it is a reminder that the last few years do not define the vastness of a potential donor's knowledge and interests.

- When someone lists every honor since being named the top safety patrol officer in sixth grade, you have someone who likes to be recognized.
- Zillow will give you an idea of what kind of house, condo, ranch, or other abode(s) your potential donor owns. This information can be misleading. Warren Buffet has never moved, and many millionaires-next-door live modestly, but Zillow does give you some geographical markers. If your donor has residences in Boston, Chicago, and Palm Desert, you have multiple places to connect. You will also get a sense that this donor has significant capacity.
- I'll never forget when a friend of mine called me after a first date saying that she really liked the guy, and that he was a lawyer, but certainly not a successful one. She felt badly about not going Dutch for dinner. He had paid $100 for his car. He didn't mention that he purchased it after his fourth car was stolen from his DuPont Circle condo in Washington, D.C. Likewise, another friend went out with

a guy in his Jaguar. Little did she know that the bank would be picking up the car the next week. Bottom line: Impressions can be deceiving.
- Ultimately, the more you know, the better. These are resources when you don't yet have a personal connection.

Here is the basic order to follow when researching a planned giving ask. I want to stress these are guidelines, not hard and fast rules. You might receive a call from an attorney saying that someone you have never heard of left your nonprofit an enormous gift, or you could work with a donor for years and never get a dime. Remember, few people, other than the very ill, feel a sense of urgency about leaving money to your nonprofit. Unlike a disaster situation when people are at immediate risk, legacy donors frequently think they have all the time in the world to make a planned giving decision. It is not like buying a refrigerator when ice cream is melting all over the place. The refrigerator buyer is not going to wait 20 years to decide.

I worked on a $40 million campaign with a colleague, Cris Wineinger, for Bermuda's one and only hospital. Bermuda is an island of 65,000 people. While there, I got on an elevator with a dentist. Floor after floor she was greeted, kissed, and hugged by everyone who entered. They were patients, friends, and relatives. When we got to our floor, I realized I was the only one who didn't know her, so I introduced myself.

It turned out she was on the board with whom I'd come to work. I asked her if there was anyone on the island she didn't know. She joked that there might be some tourists, but that the day was young. Everyone knew everyone, so using a wealth estimation program was unnecessary. Bermuda residents knew where their neighbors vacationed, who paid private tuition to what school, how much they gave and to what charities, and even how much they paid for their new boat since they also knew the seller.

The same principle is true in small towns or specific communities within a city. There are few Bosnians in St. Louis who haven't met one another. The Greek Orthodox community used to know each other quite well, but when a second church was built in the suburbs, its members went from one degree of separation to two. You don't need a search engine when you have a well-connected board.

One of the best board members I have ever met served on the foundation board of a large hospital system attached to a medical school in the Northeast. I'll call him Charles. He was the retired CEO of a large pharmaceutical company. Fellow board members said that someone Charles didn't know wasn't worth knowing. If Charles knew a person who was going to be approached, he would write up a one-page précis on the prospective donor. It was respectful and helpful. A typical précis went something like this:

"This is Larry's second marriage. He was widowed after 40 years and has been married to his second wife for two years. His first wife died at our hospital and, despite the tragic outcome, he felt she received wonderful care. He has told me multiple times that Trudy's oncologist Dr. R, cried when she died. He and his new wife have no children in common. She has a grown son who lives in California, and he has five grown children who live in New England. He was the owner of his company, which he sold two years ago. The sale price reported in *The Wall Street Journal* was $165 million. He is rough around the edges with only a high school education. A mutual friend called Larry an autodidact, which I had to look up, but it describes him perfectly. He reads everything from political treatises and *Scientific American* to *Rolling Stone*. His favorite writers are Chaucer and Doris Kearns Goodwin. He has a soft spot for single moms. His mother was widowed when he was a toddler and raised four children on her own. You should start by calling him "Mr." He likes deference. If he says, please call me Lawrence, you are in good shape. If he says, please call me Larry, you are in great shape."

And the report would go on.

Charles never wrote anything salacious. He never mentioned affairs or drug problems or any other information the donor might not want shared. People like Charles are what my late mother-in-law would call "a gem and a jewel." Information such as this from board members is invaluable, as is an introduction.

The obvious next place to expand your giving circle: your longtime donors. If you have a statewide, national, or international donor base and/or a board that is not well-connected, a search engine can be indispensable, especially if you have tens of thousands of current or potential donors.

Software should be a priority. Many small nonprofits lack the money or staff to have more than an Excel spreadsheet, but it is cheaper to purchase software than to waste the time of your board, staff, and volunteers running down rabbit holes. The groundbreaking book *The Millionaire Next Door: The Surprising Secrets of America's Wealthy,* by Thomas J. Stanley and William D. Danko, reveals how many rich and über-rich folks live under the radar. I had a meeting with a donor who had just picked up his blue blazer from the tailor. He puffed up his chest and said that it was the fifth time the tailor had relined his jacket since he bought it 23 years before. He then made a seven-figure gift. Search engines are vital to understanding the capacity of the millionaires next door.

There are also challenges with using search tools:
- They don't capture people with donor-advised funds, one of the fastest growing trends in philanthropy.
- They require the donor's home address.

- They can be expensive, although there is a fair amount of competition and the price is going down.
- Some people are very good at hiding assets.

My friend and colleague Charlie Brown is truly one of the world's great fundraisers. Decades ago, he raised $133 million for The Lawrenceville School in New Jersey. When I asked what he thinks of wealth-screening instruments, he said he finds them very useful because donors must have both capacity and generosity, two factors that guide you to a starting point.

When Charlie was consulting with San Jose State, the university had a database of 245,000 alumni, from which they were actively soliciting 186,000. There is no way you can have enough staff to meet, greet, and cultivate 186,000 people. Electronic screening is an invaluable tool to prioritize your efforts. The algorithms for projecting capacity are based on visible assets and prior gifts. The programs are not perfect, but they continue to improve in reliability. Regardless, most nonprofits still have more prospects than even a mega-team can personally solicit. Electronic screening provides a place to start.

A donor identification process that works

If you don't know the donors or potential donors, send their names to the board and long-term staff and ask if they know any of the donors personally. Hopefully, there will be notes in your software, but they might not be recent or accurate or maybe so politically correct that they are not useful. For example, I have written: "Oldest son is struggling with personal problems which are absorbing parental time, money, and concern." The non-politically correct version—that I didn't write— is: "Oldest son is doing his third stint in rehab for heroin addiction and the family is spending a small fortune on rehab and attorneys because the son also faces jail time." Never write anything you wouldn't feel comfortable with your donor reading. When you leave your position, the next person might lack these insights, but it's better to withhold highly sensitive information than to include it.

Questions to ask people who know the potential donor:

- Should I ask to speak with both the husband and wife? Remember, 82% of philanthropic decisions are made by women (*Women, Wealth and Giving* by Margaret May Damen and Niki Nicastro McCuistion). Plus, women live longer than men, and if they are included in the decision-making they may include your organization in their ultimate plans.
- What do these donors do for fun? The answer gives you a lot of information. If they participate in high-risk sports, you stress your nonprofit's history of innovation. If they are Civil War buffs, you might want to concentrate on your history of good works. If they always go to the same vacation home, stress stability. If they like to throw parties and enjoy the social circuit, talk about the people who are involved.

- Who should you bring with you? Many planned giving professionals work solo, but at times it is better to bring a wingman or, in fact, to be the wingman. It might be the person who knows the potential donor best, such as a current board member, a former physician, teacher, or client. In some cases, the CEO is the best person. Some CEOs are so insecure about the ask, that without serious coaching, or duct tape, you may have to leave the exec back at the ranch. One time, a CEO kept praising other organizations that did similar work. When asked why the donation should not be made to one of them because they were older and more established, the CEO had no response. Clearly, work needed to be done. Make sure you bring someone who is not like you. For instance, two middle-aged men who are both bankers are not as powerful a team as the mother of a client and the CEO, or a former classmate who is 60 and the development director, who is 28. One of the most powerful teams in movie history was Shirley Temple and Bill Bojangles Robinson. She was a curly-headed, five-year-old white girl, and Robinson was a middle-aged black man. They made magic when they danced together. To work with your potential donor, you need the right partner.
- Do you know why they give? This is a question you will ask during the interview, but knowledge of relationships before the meeting is invaluable. For instance, the couple might be donors because a compassionate staff person worked with their son Adam,

who subsequently died. Doing some asking about the family in the break room might enable you to say "I talked to Bess, and she sends her love. She said that Adam was really a trickster and adored watching The Three Stooges." It lets the donor know that you are interested in them and their family stories.

You might also want to set up a Google alert with your donor's name. Warning: If your donor's name is Xavier Prochaska he might be easy to find; however, if his name is Stan Smith, include the city, i.e. "Stan Smith Springfield, Missouri." I know a Dr. Xavier Prochaska who is an astrophysicist. His son has the same name. The son is in his teens and doesn't have his Ph.D. Yet. So even uncommon names can be tricky. When you get Google alerts, you have an opportunity to keep in touch with congratulations, condolences, and other kinds of cards and visits. This practice might even tip you off when donors sell a business.

Research before a visit—doing your homework

Wealth-screening software programs are not infallible. They do not capture the names of members of an extended family with a family foundation. They don't capture the people who have donor-advised funds. My family has a small donor-advised fund. An invitation to a stewardship event was addressed to the gift officer who manages our fund. She forwarded the invitation to us and we responded yes. When we arrived at the event, an overzealous volunteer blocked us from entering saying, "The gift was from the YouthBridge Foundation, not from you. And you are not Barbara Carswell (our gift officer's name)." It was an outdoor event on a hot day, so we left. We will still give, because we believe in the charity, but the experience left a bad taste in our mouths. We have not included the organization in our estate plan. This is the kind of information my friends and family know, but not a search engine.

When I asked a wealth search engine salesperson for a demonstration, I suggested a search on my family. We are the sort of family that is problematic for search engines. My husband is Frank Edward Robbins IV; our son, Frank Edward Robbins V; and our grandson, Frank Edward Robbins VI. All have used our address at one time or another. My name is Carol Elaine Weisman. We adopted our niece at age 16. Guess what her name is? Carol Ruth Weisman! And neither of us use our middle name. The donor-advised fund was not on the search engine's radar at all. It also showed that we had loans from graduate school. This would be pathetic, as my husband is retired, but our son had just finished grad school. Ultimately, the search suggested that we were good for an ask of about $250. I was thrilled, but I am sure a charity that searched us would not be happy with the information, because our capacity is somewhat more.

Your best source of information will frequently be your board members or staff who have worked with the family. Here is an example of not listening:

A colleague of mine I'll call Denise was on the board of a cycling organization. Being a professional fundraiser for more than 20 years, she knew a lot about how to ask. Her children had gone to the same school as the couple's kids and she knew them fairly well. She set up coffee with the couple who were already annual donors. She called the development director, who we'll call Jeff. Denise asked that they set up a meeting to talk strategy.

Jeff: Don't worry, I've met them, done a wealth screen. I've got this.

Denise: There are probably some things you don't know.

Jeff: Really, I've got this. I've got to run to a meeting.

Denise: At least meet me 10 minutes before our coffee.

Jeff: Of course. You're the expert. (Denise detected a distinct note of snottiness in his tone.)

Denise: I've been friends with them for over 25 years. We raised our children together. There's a bond between women who have carpooled together for years, not unlike combat buddies.

Jeff: Right. I'm sure you're right. As I said, I've got to run.

Later, they met at the coffee shop. Jeff said that since he and the donor were both century cyclists (meaning they had cycled a hundred miles or more in a day) he would lead with that.

Denise informed Jeff that the couple had three children. The oldest girl, a freshman in college, was tall and willowy like the Dad and runway-ready. The second daughter was 5'5" and 75 lbs. overweight. The mother categorized the younger daughter as severely obese and said she had already booked a bariatric surgery consultation. Despite her weight, the daughter was on the high school tennis team. The mother obsessed about her daughter's weight. Denise usually cringed when she asked her friend how things were going, because she frequently answered, "Sarah is still fat. How good could I be?" The mother constantly monitored her own weight while daily harassing her 17-year-old daughter about her food intake. The third child was a 13-year-old boy who was a major geek. He spent hours building computers and programming them. He was stick-thin.

Denise suggested, therefore, that they start with the program for inner city kids to receive bikes and become active. Jeff said that he would prefer to do things his way.

After 40 minutes of cycling talk, the couple was obviously bored and the wife was collecting her purse and coat. She said that they were giving to Syrian refugees and that having to walk 2,000 miles was a lot more important than cycling a hundred miles. Denise finally said, "But it is not more important than our children not living as long as we will because of inactivity, which leads to heart disease, diabetes and, from what you've told me, an increased risk of cancer." The wife put her purse back down, and they closed the sale.

The couple later included this organization in their estate plan. The mother of three told Denise, "There will always be refugees, and we need to support them, but we can't let this be the first generation of Americans who are outlived by their parents. If I could only get Sarah to walk a couple of thousand miles!"

Lessons learned:

- Listen to the folks who know your potential donor.
- When working with a partner, decide who is going to do what before you go.
- Know what is important to your potential donors.

Summary

There are multiple ways to research your potential donor. Friends, family, and colleagues of the donor tell a very different story than search engines. Both are powerful tools in creating your planned giving strategy.

DON'T AMBUSH PROSPECTS

5

How to ask

Many people are not comfortable asking for a planned gift. You may think that you will be focusing on death, and, if you do, that can certainly feel intrusive. But in fact, asking for a planned gift is about instilling optimism and fulfilling your donor's dreams to create a better future.

How you communicate, whether in writing or on the phone or face-to-face, is critical.

- Make the call to set up the appointment. You might also write a note or email first and then follow up with a call. Whatever works, keep doing it. If this is a first-time cultivation meeting, you might want to meet at a restaurant, coffee shop, or bar. (If you meet at a bar, you are going to order a coke or club soda or wine spritzer!) If this is an ask meeting, the donor's home is a much better place. Some of these guidelines vary by city and custom. You are, for example, far less likely to meet in a home in New York City than in Des Moines, Iowa. Travel time is a real issue in New York. The advantage of meeting in a home is that you have privacy and if the donor is well known you don't have the interruption of friends, staff, or waiters. Do not ask: Would you like to meet? Ask: Would you be available Tuesday or Thursday next week?

- Dr. James Oldroyd of MIT advises that the best time to call a prospect is between 4-5 p.m. on a Wednesday or Thursday. This research was not done on nonprofit giving prospects but is nonetheless noteworthy. Ask the donor what is most convenient. Give options: Would you like to meet at our agency, your home or office, or a restaurant? If the potential donor or couple has a disability, ask if s(he) would like a ride. One development director in the Washington, D.C. area, closed a six-figure ask at a Roy Rogers (comparable to an Arby's or McDonalds). This restaurant was the elderly donor's favorite place, but her daughters wouldn't take her there because of the sodium-laden vittles.

- If you know the donor and are going to ask for a planned gift, say, "In addition to yourself, is there anyone else involved in your philanthropic decision-making we should include?" This might be an adult child, financial advisor, estate-planning attorney, or friend. I worked with a group of older Catholic women. About 95% had never worked outside the home and about 75% were widows. Many kept the household accounts, but did not deal with large gifts, investments, or purchases without conferring with a spouse. Almost all wanted to bring someone to the meeting. My husband was once asked for a donation by the head of the school where our son attended. He said, "I am totally middle management. You have to talk to my wife." Everyone is different, which is why questions rather than assumptions will produce better results.

- Schedule a strategy meeting with the person who is going to accompany you. Always meet at least 15 minutes before the meeting and get the chitchat out of the way. You don't want to go into the meeting asking your partner where she parked or when she is having her hip replaced. You want to focus on the donor. Decide what questions you want to ask, whether this is a cultivation, an ask, or a stewardship call. If it is an ask, decide who is going to do it and for how much. Be prepared to be nimble. The donor might be ready to give on the first meeting or may not decide for five or more years. I remember hiring a realtor suggested by my friend Susan. Susan's house had been on the market for three years, so, frustrated, she hired a new agent, who sold her house in two weeks. When I met with the successful real estate agent when selling a condo, she kept trying to sell me on her services. Finally I said, "You're hired. I don't care who's in your office. I've heard about Susan's house and other difficult properties you've sold. My condo should be a piece of cake." And it was. Listen closely, someone might have already decided to give on a first meeting.

- It is not unheard of for a donor to want to give a restricted gift that you really don't want. A restricted gift is one that can only be used for the purpose outlined in a letter of agreement. An unrestricted gift is one that can be used in any manner the nonprofit sees fit. If it is something you really don't want, such as funding for a ballet program for a food pantry, you might need to regroup. You don't want to say "no" outright. It is painful to turn down money, but mission creep is not acceptable either. So sometimes you just must say, "Great idea. Let me take it back to the board and get back to you." This gives you time to regroup.

The basic choreography of an ask

- Start with a thank you such as, "You have been giving your money, your skills, and your time— or all three—to our organization for 17 years. We can't thank you enough for your generosity and loyalty." Be as specific as possible. You might say, "This is the 15th anniversary year of your first gift." Or, "Younger volunteers are inspired by your 55 years of volunteering at our church's preschool. Helen Vitale, one of our newest volunteers, told me yesterday how much she admires your skills and commitment. She said she'd learned a lot from you."

- Do *not* start with your story. You might give to a charity because your grandmother died of emphysema. Your potential donor might have emphysema and be very much alive and not want to hear your story about a death from the same disease. The couple you are talking to might be childless, and not by choice. When talking about the future, it is very different for people without children. Phrases like "The world the next generation will inherit" might not resonate with the childless crowd, whether childless by choice or not. Next question, and always ask permission: "May we ask why you give to us?" You might already know, for instance, that this person graduated from your educational institution, so the question would be "I know that you are a 1967 graduate. However, with all the wonderful organizations out there, how were we fortunate enough to be one of your charities?" Now, listen *very* carefully. What the donor says next is gold. If she says, "Your hospital took incredibly good care of my mother. She did not survive her renal disease, but we couldn't have asked for better care." During your close, you might want to ask the donor if she would like a fund named for, in honor of, or in memory of Mom. Or, if the doctor was reported to be of great significance or exuded compassionate care, ask about honoring the physician. If the potential planned giver says, "I was going through a divorce and working two jobs. Had it not been for the Boys and Girls Club, my son would probably be dead, like his cousin who joined a gang that was pressuring my son to join." You then make an empathic remark: "That must have been a terrible time in your life." Then ask the question, "In what way did our Boys and Girls Club help your son?" Again, *listen*. If it was sports, that is your hook. If it was academics, that is your closer.

- Link the program focus of your organization to the reason for giving that your donor has shared. "We are seeing a lot more adolescent suicide attempts in our community. Your daughter's experience losing her best friend to suicide was obviously traumatic for your whole family. The fact that the parents tried to get her help and there was no place to go is tragic. We have only 25 in-patient beds for adolescents and 100 slots for outpatient care in our whole city, and as you've seen, the need is so much greater." *Then stop talking.* Listen for the "phrase that pays": What can be done? What would it cost? How can I help?

- Do not brag about your work without expressing a need. "Our little theater won a regional Tony last year and we couldn't be more thrilled, but maybe you heard about the night the air conditioning went out. Our building is on the historic register because of its significance and beauty, but the infrastructure needs major updating. And this will continue to be an issue." *Then stop talking.* For the close, the most powerful phrase you can use is: "Would you join me in putting our charity in your estate plan or with a gift today?" *Then stop talking.*

- If there are questions you can't answer, there is no problem. You tell the donor that you know just the right person who has the answers and you will have them follow up. I have a friend whose husband asked if he could name a building for $5,000. The gift officer was smart enough to say, "Let me have a little time and see what your gift could accomplish." You ask for their preferred means of communication and the best time to reach them. In my friend's case, her husband received a list of things that could be named for $5,000, such as a bench or two stadium seats. He also got a list of the actual naming rights for a building or a visiting professorship. The planned giving officer then came back to him and asked about possibly purchasing an insurance policy. Since the donor had heart disease, diabetes, and few of his original parts, this idea did not seem like a workable scenario. This conversation took place about five years ago. To the credit of the gift officer, he sends a birthday card every year and calls at least once a year to update the potential donor on activities in his area of interest. (His wife and children gave him a named stadium seat for his 75th birthday.)

- Ask the donor if (s)he would like to make the gift in honor of someone important in the donor's life. It can be a parent, child, sibling, mentor, friend, or professional who volunteered or worked at the nonprofit. Or, as I learned from Hand in Paw in Birmingham, Alabama, it can be a pet.
- Thank the donor, hit the road, and, if you were working with a partner, debrief. If you received a fabulous response, celebrate (I prefer carbs to booze, but that is up to you!). If, however, the ask went off the rails, you may have to debrief the next day to give yourself time to process it. Warning: Glide out the door after a big win. Once, a friend and I started dancing and singing in the elevator after an unexpectedly large gift when the donor called. He heard everything. Fortunately, he was amused. A colleague made a visit to an ophthalmologist about a planned gift. The doctor knew that this meeting was an ask. He made it clear that without the head of the division of ophthalmology there would be no meeting. The planned giving officer was salivating. The potential donor then went into a hysterical rant about the medical school sending a van to his area, more than 45 minutes from the med school, to take seniors from an adult day care for free cataract exams. He accused the school of stealing his patients, and most of the rest of what he said cannot be printed. He demanded an end to the practice of giving free rides and exams and wanted

a written apology. The planned giving officer said she was trembling by the time she left and ran to her car. Eventually the dean of the medical school got involved in the controversy and the planned giving officer said, "Call me when this is resolved. This is totally above my pay grade."

- Write up the call in your database, including next steps. Call anyone who needs to follow up.
- Write a thank-you note. If you have illegible handwriting, I give you permission (as if I am the boss of you) to type; otherwise, handwritten is better. Email is not acceptable. Your note should read something like this:

Dear Kim and Paul,

I can't stop thinking about the story of how you met 35 years ago—on the parking lot of our symphony hall during a snowstorm when Kim's car wouldn't start.

We so appreciate your loyalty and your love of symphonic music. I am going to take your advice and give Mahler another listen.

And again, thank you for including us in your estate plan. Generations of audiences will hear both the new and experimental music you love, as well as the classics, such as Bach and Dvorak, that we all adore.

Sincerely,

Judy Smith, MBA
Director, Planned Giving

- Send a gift acceptance letter for signature.
- Check back in the agreed-upon period and ask if they need any help or information getting the estate gift prepared. If you are part of a national organization or if local organizations have similar names, make sure they get the name right.
- Steward them until they die! Then steward their relatives who might be interested in your organization. You'll find the section on stewardship in chapter 7.

Sometimes an unusual ask will work

I was working with a group in cattle-ranching country. I was sitting next to the daughter of another board member. She told me how her father made not only a major gift but also a pledge for a planned gift. Her father was a short guy, maybe 5'3". I was shocked to hear that five board members came to him to ask for the capital gift. Her father turned around and said that it was nine men. He continued the story about how they were all committed to the cause and had already made their gifts. I asked if he didn't think he was being ganged up on. He said, "Just the opposite. I was honored that they had all taken off work to come see me." I would never have recommended sending such a large group, but I would have been wrong.

Periodically, I think my clients do things just to teach me a lesson. A woman I'll call Susie is a case in point.

Her nonprofit had never done a campaign, in fact, had not done much more than an annual appeal that raised around $10,000-$15,000 and some small events that grossed $20,000-$30,000. I kept trying to convince her to do a feasibility study, and she kept telling me that they didn't have the money for one. (I don't do feasibility studies, so this had nothing to do with selling my services.) The nonprofit wanted to raise $1.5 million. Two weeks after my droning on about the importance of a feasibility study, Susie called me. She was 40+, but, like the cheerleader she once was, she gushed in her excited, slightly high-pitched voice, "I was at Starbucks this morning. I took my son in early for band practice, but had some time and you know how I love my morning chai latte. I ran into a guy I knew in high school. He asked me what I was up to and I told him all about the great work we were doing. He asked me to stay and chat. Well, Carol, it turns out he and his brothers had just sold their company the night before and wanted to put some money back into the community. He called both of his brothers while we had our coffee and they are giving us a million dollars."

I mean really. Getting a mill at Starbucks by a chance meeting! Susie then coyly asked if we still needed a feasibility study. Sheepishly, I said no. It is noteworthy that all three brothers were on the annual appeal list and had never given a dime.

Why did this work?
- She knew the donor.

- He was searching for a philanthropic investment.
- She was glowing with enthusiasm and promise.
- She clearly was going to be in a leadership position and the brothers felt confident that the work would get done.

I wouldn't spend a lot of time at Starbucks hoping to run into a newly minted millionaire, but it worked for Susie.

When we discussed next steps, she said that the "boys" would probably have a lot of spare time now that they had sold their business. She decided to ask the brother with a law degree to chair the capital campaign. She also planned to recruit the other two either to join the board or chair the annual gala. Down the road, she'd ask for a planned gift.

What is the best source of information on your donors? Friends and family. Sometimes they are right about a prospect, and sometimes they are not. But always listen closely. Few of us know exactly how much money a friend has or what he or she cares about.

Asking a group of people

Almost all nonprofits meet occasionally, even if they have an international membership. The schedule can be packed, so addressing your potential donors must be done well, whether one-on-one or in a large setting. Ideally, planned giving will be the primary topic, but this is not always possible.

What to include in a planned giving speech and who should give it

Above all, your speaker should be someone who has *made* a planned gift, not a pledge to make a gift.

Other requirements:

- Someone who is a good speaker or willing to get training. The question I ask the self-proclaimed good speakers is, "What is your standing ovation rate?" Dianne Belk, who speaks to potential donors for the Girl Scouts, is at around a 90% standing ovation rate. I am happy with 35%. If your speaker says zero or just looks puzzled, there is room for improvement.
- A speaker who is respectful of time. Writing the following five-minute speech took me six weeks. I am a marathoner, not a sprinter. A short speech is much more difficult than a long one. As Mark Twain once said, "I wish I'd had time to write a shorter letter."
- Someone who has a story to tell about how your organization has impacted his or her life.

An example of a short ask speech

This is a speech I wrote for my high school alumni foundation. The schedule was packed so I was lucky to get any time. I knew that the first speaker, who was in his mid-30s, had won a Pulitzer Prize. I am starting to get used to following dynamic speakers who are younger than my children, but this was really intimidating. Here is my five-minute ask:

"It is not just great to be standing in front of you today. It is amazing. Not only did I not win a Pulitzer like the previous speaker, I graduated from Ladue with a 2.6 average. I went on to the University of Denver. For those of you who do not know this esteemed institution, in 1967, when I entered, *Playboy Magazine* would not rank D.U. as a party school because the magazine did not rank amateurs with professionals. Because of the education I received at Ladue and despite not taking any advanced placement classes, I tested out of a year of college and with summer school, graduated in two and a half years and went on to receive two master's degrees from Washington University, which is frankly nobody's idea of a party school.

"What I loved about Ladue is that it is great for almost everyone. My younger sister Nancy was a National Merit Finalist, a National Science Foundation Winner, and Betty Crocker Homemaker of the Year. She went to Brown University for undergrad and attended medical school at Columbia. Ferguson shooting victim Michael Brown's mother, Lezley McSpadden, was a classmate of my son. She shared what a great experience she had at Ladue in her book, *Tell the Truth and Shame the Devil*.

"I'll never forget eavesdropping on my parents arguing about where to send me to high school. My mother said, "Carol is absolutely not going to Mary Institute. I will not have my daughter grow up to be a French-speaking debutante." Frankly, Mom was wrong. I know many of those Mary Institute "girls" today. They are my neighbors and friends, and, the truth is, few of them speak French.

"But times have changed. If I had a 12-year-old daughter today, thanks to a $100 million-dollar capital campaign, I'd consider sending her to Mary Institute (now called MICDS), which has one of the top science programs in the country.

"We need to keep up. That is why I have not only made a gift to the capital campaign for the high school renovations, but also have included The Ladue Education Foundation in my estate plan. I hope you will join me in a capital and planned gift.

"In the meantime, I will go home to my French-speaking husband and wait for the Pulitzer committee to call."

When you host an event

Consider making planned giving the focus of one of your events. If you have a wide array of topics, then the planned giving opportunity will not stand out. This event can take place in a home with a small number of people, at a local, national or international conference with hundreds of people, or at an annual meeting. There should be time to talk and relax. You might already know your donors, or this event will give you a chance to know them better. Notice who they talk to and who on your board might be a friend or acquaintance.

Depending on the city and the date, you will know how to attract the greatest turnout. In some cities without traffic issues, 5-6:30 pm works; in other places, a morning or lunch meeting is better for avoiding rush hour. Be aware of issues such as childcare for young parents or night driving for the older crowd. If you cannot dedicate an event for planned giving, at least mention it at every event you do host and honor those who belong to your legacy society. When peers see that "the smart money" is giving, it can be highly motivating.

Train your champion, aka your best and most articulate and respected advocate, point person, spokesperson, savior—you get the picture. Your champion needs to share his or her story, explain why s(he) has made a planned gift, and describe his or her vision of the future. To get speaker training, you might want to look for a Certified Speaking Professional (CSP) in your city and ask for a few hours of pro bono coaching. A CSP is the highest-earned designation by the National Speakers Association and requires at least 50 speeches a year for no less than five years, for a minimum of 100 clients and for a minimum combined income of $250,000. I have never been turned down when I've asked for help with a client, except when there was a time crunch, in which case another CSP was recruited.

The speech needs to be factual, personal, poignant, and donor-focused, with a call to action at the end. It also must be carefully timed, no longer than 20-30 minutes, depending on the crowd. Ideally, have your champion write the speech, present it to a safe group, such as your board or staff, videotape it, review it, and make edits. This is a high-stakes speech, not a casual, off-the-cuff chat. I also recommend Toastmasters for trying out segments of a speech. Plus, you never know. Members of your Toastmasters group could become planned givers!

The speech must be tailored to your audience. You might have a core presentation, but it must be geared so that this crowd finds your issue important to them. You might start with, "As mothers and grandmothers of students at our school... or, as a financial management professional... or, when you were 16, how many of you remember cutting as being an issue?" (Cutting, also called self-injury, is the act of deliberately harming the surface of one's body.) You need to know who will be in the audience before you arrive. When speaking to a wealthy group, you might mention discussing a gift with their financial advisors. You might not want to assume that a more middle-class audience has financial advisors, donor-advised funds, or family foundations.

Speaker Introduction: This is an important but frequently overlooked aspect of a dynamic presentation. The introduction should make people clamor to hear the speaker. It should share why this person has "the privilege of the platform," or, in other words, why you should be listening. It should include:

The speaker's relationship to the mission. For instance, is the presenter a professional in the field, a former or current client, or the parent or spouse of a client?

The speaker's accomplishments that are relevant to the audience. A Nobel Prize is always worth mentioning, but if you are speaking to a group from your place of worship, the awards your speaker has won for productivity from his or her employer might not be germane.

A few personal facts such as hobbies, number of children, etc.

If the speaker has an accent (all of us do outside our hometown) always mention where the speaker was born or the audience will use up brainpower wondering whether this person is British, South African, or Australian.

A sample introduction

"It is a great pleasure to welcome our guest speaker, Cynthia Frohlichstein. Cynthia is a 43-year breast cancer survivor. She is here to tell her story of going from victim to survivor to champion. She also wants to share her deep belief that having boobs is not a predictor of romance. She had her first date with the love of her life the night before she went in for what she thought was a biopsy and turned out to be a double mastectomy. Five months later, they were married.

"Cynthia is an award-winning journalist, who has written everything from travel articles to children's books. Her latest book, "The Peanut Butter Kid," is for sale at the back of the room after her talk. Proceeds go to breast cancer research.

"Cynthia is the mother of two and a grandmother. Though she deeply misses her husband of 42 years, Harvey Frohlichstein, who recently passed away, she continues to be grateful for her 43 years of being cancer-free. Let's give a warm New Jersey welcome to Cynthia Frohlichstein."

Hints:

- Write the introduction on blue card stock so that it won't get lost and use at least 18-point type so that the person who is doing the introduction can easily read it.

- Have the person giving the introduction wait on the stage or at the front of the room, shake hands, and start a round of applause. This sets up your speaker for success.
- Customize the introduction to the audience. If, for example, Cynthia were speaking at the hospital where she had her surgery, mention how grateful she was for the care she received. If she were speaking to an audience of journalists, cite her writing awards.
- Venue: Make sure everyone can sit. My husband looks great, but after eight orthopedic surgeries he can't stand for long periods. He feels like a jerk when he sits and an older woman stands (he is of that era.) I once gave a speech in a woman's living room that sat 80. (This was Dallas, so no real surprise.) Visit the residence to make sure the seating is adequate. Also, ask the hostess if there are any special requests. Many people prefer not to serve red wine because of its potential to stain carpeting and furniture.

Be very clear who is paying for what. A clarifying email is important and would read something like this:

Dear Susan,

Thank you so much for agreeing to host an "at home" for our organization. We really appreciate your offer to pay for the food and drinks. As you requested, the invitations will say, "Hosted by Susan and Terry Block," rather than the original Mr. and Mrs. Terry Block. We will have a list of guests for your concierge. We are expecting no more than 36 people including staff. We will get you the final number at least three days before the event. We will bring typewritten nametags and the handouts. Please let us know what time we should arrive and anything else we can do to aid your magnanimous support of our city's children living with juvenile diabetes.

Many thanks,

Patti Christin
Director of Development

If you expect a large crowd, you might want to look for a country club or hotel or other public venue. I don't like using a hospital meeting room or church basement. I believe that a place that is comfortable and upscale gives the feeling of abundance and promise.

I would avoid the great outdoors. I once spoke in a beautiful park in Florida. The evening was balmy, the lights were twinkling, and the bugs were feasting. It was the first time I have ever seen cans of bug spray on the refreshment tables. It became so uncomfortable the host wisely suggested I make my talk 20 minutes instead of 40. Between bugs, rain, snow, and frequently an inadequate sound system, it's better to host indoors.

Also, make sure your venue is handicapped-accessible. One of my clients uses the term "TAB," as in "Temporarily Able-Bodied," to describe most people. Many of us have had orthopedic problems, whether we broke a leg skiing or a fall down some stairs. Some folks have neurological or other chronic conditions, and some are our wounded warriors. It is smart, considerate, and appreciated to have an accessible venue. If it is a house, and someone is in a wheelchair, make sure you can get the chair into the house and to a bathroom.

Food and drinks: Food has become a challenging political and health issue. I come from a pretty typical family: I've had celiac disease since I was six months old (way before it was cool!), plus diabetes; my daughter-in-law is allergic to shrimp; one son is a vegetarian; my husband's brother has been in recovery for 25+ years (way to go, George!); and the list goes on. If it is a lunch, make it light. I once spoke in Manchester, England, where we were served a lunch of prime rib, Yorkshire pudding, an enormous trifle, plus wine. It was not my most alert audience! You might consider a buffet because there are more choices. Always have soft drinks or sparkling waters if you are serving alcohol. I was a speaker at a French cultural event where all the drinks were alcoholic. The food was to die for, but for people in recovery, for Mormons, Seventh-day Adventists, Muslims, and others with religious strictures on drinking, for people driving, or, in my case, for a speaker trying to give a cogent talk, at least break out some bottled or sparkling water.

Additional Suggestions

- Have staff, board, and volunteers wear badges so that they can clearly be identified. Give them specific tasks such as greeting people at the door. I spoke at a very elegant event at the Four Seasons in St. Louis for Rainbow Village, which provides housing for adults with developmental disabilities. One of the residents, who later was awarded the title of "Mayor of Rainbow Village," gave me the warmest greeting I have ever received. He was charm personified.

- If it is very dark when you finish or if it is cold and icy, ask staff or volunteers to help older donors to their cars. (You lose points when your guests break a hip!) Always consider valet parking if the venue calls for it.
  - Educate your staff how to interact with your guests. Give them guidelines on dress code and alcohol consumption. Suggest ways to circulate and make introductions, including their own. Make it clear whether they are at the event to work the crowd or to enjoy themselves as guests. If they are there to meet and greet, spend some time role-playing.
  - Have a 10-minute briefing for board, staff, and volunteers about what information should be shared with donors. A "cheat sheet" with three to five points can be helpful.

Logistics and other details

- Ensure that your champion is prepared and comfortable with directions to the event. Be considerate of overnight lodging or transportation that may be necessary. Note: Not everyone is comfortable driving at night.
- Obtain your champion's introduction. Help write it if necessary. Be careful of academics who have a 90-page curriculum vitae with every paper they've written or full-time volunteers who might be self-conscious about not having a college degree. Review the introduction with your champion and get an okay. If his or her name is difficult to pronounce, and you are not doing the introduction, spell it phonetically and rehearse with the person doing the introduction.
- If your speaker is flying in for the event, be clear who is paying for what. Dianne Belk and her husband Lawrence Calder graciously foot their own expenses. If your champion is not able to do so, be clear before you even begin. Many years ago, I was on a national board that had a big-time fundraising event at the Metropolitan Museum of Art. One of the hottest celebrities in Hollywood was invited to cut the ribbon. She not only flew first class from L.A., but her husband came as a surprise from London, where he was filming. She brought an entourage for hair and makeup, plus a personal

assistant and a secretary. The total expenses for her "free" appearance was around $17,000, and this was in 1980. Again, clarity is the name of the game, and put who is responsible for what *in writing.*

After the event, follow up with a phone call from the person who knows the guest the best. It might be a staff person, board member, volunteer, or the champion. I prefer a call to a letter because there is two-way communication and private questions can be answered. There is no problem if the person who calls does not know the answers to specific questions. The caller might then say, "I really should know that. Would you like me to have our CFO or program manager call you?"

Here is a script for the call:

- Introduce yourself: "This is Kristin Wild. I am the executive director of the Ladue Education Foundation.
- State the reason for your call: "I would love to get some feedback on our program and answer any questions you might have."
- Arrange for follow-up. This might be a tour or a call from a staff person who is skilled at the subtleties of complex planned gifts, or it might be a meeting with a financial advisor, attorney, spouse, parent, or child.
- If no follow-up is necessary, thank the guest.
- If appropriate, follow up with a personal card that mentions something interesting the person said.

After one event, I called a woman who was a major donor in the past to thank her for attending. She said that she only came because she wanted to get out of the house. She shared that she was giving only to breast cancer; because her mother had died of it three years before, she herself was a survivor, and her daughter was having prophylactic removal of both breasts the following week. I expressed my concerns and wished her well and didn't mention my charity again. I then sent a $10 gift in her daughter's name to a breast cancer charity in honor of a speedy recovery. Two months later, a large check arrived with a note from the donor that said, "There is more to life than breasts!" When I left the board, I put a note in the database for the development professional to discuss a planned gift and, in the meantime, to stay in touch.

Overcoming objections

Surprise, surprise, not everyone will have the insight, the vision, the heart, or the knowledge to immediately say yes.

One of the best fundraising board members I have ever known is a woman I mentioned in Chapter One who had been severely abused as a child. I'll call her Regina. She weighed 340 at age 24. While her brother spent more than half his life in prison, she turned her life around thanks to a caring mentor. Regina earned a college degree, lost 210 lbs., became the top salesperson in the U.S. for a large computer firm, married a rich guy, and joined a child abuse prevention board. One of the other board members was scared senseless about making an ask. Regina put her hand on the frightened member's shoulder and said, "Oh, honey, believe me, you can survive someone saying no to you. The fact is, no one is going to hit you." Truer words were never spoken. I've heard no stories of violence when asking for a planned or a major gift.

Knowing what to do makes all the difference. Some people say to just brush off a rejection. I am not so sure that is wise. I think you must spend some time analyzing why someone said no and decide if the rejection might have had something to do with you and not with the other person. The most common mistake when asking is talking too much. You can go back later and ask for feedback:

- Was it the timing?
- Was it the cause?
- Was it something I said?

The newer you are at asking, the more likely your potential donor will be honest. Here are some responses to objections:

Donor: "I just don't know."
You: "What are your concerns?" *Then listen.*
Donor: "I can't make up my mind."
You: "What have I left unclear?" *Then listen.*
Donor: "I'm not ready to give."

You: "When would be a good time to get back to you?" *Then listen.*

Follow-up question: "What means of communication do you prefer?"

Donor: "NO!"

You: "May I ask why?" *Then listen.*

Donor: "I have to talk to my wife first."

You: "When would it be convenient for us to talk together?" *Then listen.*

Donor: "Can I give restricted funds?"

You: "What are you interested in?" *Then listen.*

Donor: "I don't make bequests. All my money is going to my children."

You: "How do you like to give?" *Then listen.*

Sometimes you never find out the real reason someone declined. And sometimes you do. One of my clients asked a fellow alum for a large gift and got a resounding no, which he took personally since they had been fraternity brothers. A year later, the client found out his frat brother had declared bankruptcy shortly after their conversation. My client was a smart guy. And a kind guy. He called and apologized for not following up and asked if he could help his fellow alum to get back on his feet.

Summary

Whoever asks should already have made a planned gift. Different situations require different strategies. In a one-on-one meeting, the job of the solicitor is to ask questions. If it is a large venue, the task is to convey a poignant and compelling story and include an ask and information on how to give. In both situations, follow-up is crucial.

WE'D LIKE TO TELL YOU ABOUT OUR EXCITING NEW BUILDING PROJECT!

6

Who should make the ask

Having a professional planned giving staff makes the process much, much easier for board, volunteers, and other development personnel in that they know the technical aspects of planned giving. You are ready to invest money and time in a full-blown planned giving program *if*:

- You have been in business 10 years or more.
- Your nonprofit has recognized and respected leaders.
- You have a strong donor base.
- You have a commitment from your board.
- Your donor retention rate is at least 50-60%.
- People have shared that you are already in their estate plan.
- You have the bandwidth to set up your brokerage account and have gift acceptance policies in place.

- You have received an unsolicited planned gift. It is thought that about one-third of all planned givers have never donated a gift to the organization in their lifetime. Because of special events, I am not sure this is true. A planned giver could have come to an event or been a guest at a corporate table or played golf as the guest of a friend for years and you might not have any information. Or your surprise donor might have given to you through a federated payroll deduction such as the United Way or the Jewish Federation.

Indications you are *not* ready for a planned giving program
- You don't have at least two months of expenses in the bank.
- You don't have a champion on the board to promote planned giving.
- You have less than $500,000 in donor income excluding special events, and you are not ready to launch a full-blown planned giving campaign that would include hiring staff. This is a somewhat controversial figure, as there are pros and cons to starting a planned giving program before reaching this number.

You ultimately need to plant tomatoes *and* acorns. Planting tomatoes gives a quick yield. With an acorn, you must wait a very, very long time to sit under the shade and relax. I am suggesting that you do both.

If you are not ready for a full-blown planned giving program, here are the steps to get there within the next few years:

- Gather the full contact information on guests attending your events. If you sold tables, the only information you might have is the name of the corporation or single donor, such as John Deere or Mr. and Mrs. Harvey Brown. Ideally, you want the following information from everyone at the table: cell phone numbers, email addresses, and home addresses. The reason you want a home address is that when you research the giving potential of a donor, current search engine tools require a home address. One great blessing of cell phones is that few, if any of us, plan to change our numbers. Every piece of communication should have a line about planned giving and contact information. If you have a small staff and no development professional, try to find a board or community foundation member with financial acumen to answer any questions. You can also consider using a for-profit financial institution. Be aware that many want a minimum-sized fund, and if you are just starting out you might not reach this threshold. Be very clear in your communications how a planned gift should be made. This is particularly important for organizations with local and national chapters. There has been more than one battle between a national and local chapter if the name of the receiving organization is ambiguous. To avoid this problem, share your legal name in all communications. Likewise, suggest that your donor consider giving unrestricted funds. My husband, Frank, and I included a Unitarian retreat center called Star Island in our estate plan. Twenty years ago, we wouldn't have thought about the opportunity to install solar energy or the work and money that would be needed to meet compliance for Homeland Security. We trust the leadership to make wise choices. This will not appeal to your donors with control issues! When you bring on new board members, ask them: Do you have a will? If so, have you included charitable gifts? Is our organization one of them? Do *not* push people for this information if they feel uncomfortable sharing it, especially if the person has been recruited with limited knowledge of your organization. It is always powerful to say, "I have *our* organization in my estate plan. As you get to know us, I hope you will join me as a legacy donor." If the new board member does not have an estate plan but is interested, suggest at least two or three estate planning attorneys. You don't want your nonprofit to appear as a pipeline for a specific lawyer. Put your planned giving acceptance policy in place. There is a lot of boilerplate, which is easily available if you are part of a national organization. A former teacher of mine tried to donate his hand-hooked rugs to an art museum. When a staff person told him that by their standards his work was not art, he was hurt that the museum didn't want them. (I didn't want them either!) What the museum didn't do was share its specific policy that prevented them from accepting the gift. The museum also failed to offer him an alternative, such as a craft museum. The result? He changed his will to delete his gift to the museum. I helped him after heart surgery, and he left me a lava lamp from the 1960s that I had admired—for me, the perfect gift.

Hiring Staff

Nonprofit board members often harbor the fantasy that they will hire staff to do all the fundraising, while they themselves will dabble on the program side or, better still, without any training, supervise the development professionals.

A planned giving expert should never be your first hire, because planned giving is a long-term strategy. When you reach certain benchmarks, however, it is time to hire staff. These benchmarks include:

- A successful capital campaign of $1 million or more
- At least 1,000 annual donors
- A business operating for 10 years or more
- A senior executive (sometimes called executive director, president, or CEO) for a minimum of one year
- A cause that lends itself easily to planned gifts. For instance, a Montessori school, which serves children ages two through 12, is more difficult than a

senior living community that serves people 65 to the end of life.

These rules are not hard and fast. It is a little like baking bread. When you make bread, you sprinkle a clean, stable surface with flour. You scrape the dough out of the bowl onto this surface and scrape the bowl and your fingers clean of sticky strands of dough. Then you push the dough down and out, stretching it flat in front of you with the heels of your hands till it feels "right." Every situation is slightly different whether you use a different kind of wheat, knead with a higher percentage of moisture in the air, or cook at a different altitude. The same is true of planned giving. Some of it is science and some of it is feel. You might have a new major gift officer with a lot of planned giving experience. You might find someone who wants to make matching gifts. Or, you might come upon a funder willing to do a capacity-building grant to get you started. Suffice it to say, it takes muscle, patience, and time.

What skills and personality traits to look for in a planned giving professional:

- Someone who is a good listener. While a charismatic leader can excite a crowd, a one-to-one setting means listening to the donor, not preaching about your mission or the greatness of your organization.
- Someone who can make complex concepts understandable to laymen. Once you get into the alphabet soup of planned giving options, a donor can easily

get confused. One family member might understand everything immediately, but another might be baffled. Your planned giving officer needs to make sure everyone in the room is on the same page.
- Someone who likes people. A professional will see the best and sometimes the worst in others. S(he) will need to assume that people want to do the best they can. With divorces, multiple marriages, and disenfranchised children among your donors, your planned giving professional will periodically need skills normally held only by therapists, bartenders, and hairdressers.
- Someone who is a team player. The planned giving expert works with other development staff and program folks and will frequently meet with attorneys, financial planners, spouses, adult children, and any number of other people your donor wants involved in the decision-making process.
- Someone who is optimistic. Seeing a brighter future and the chance to make major changes or give significant support to a cause the donor cherishes is all-important.
- Someone who looks and behaves like a professional. Yes, that might mean wearing a tie and dress shoes—no flip flops!—staying sober during meals, and generally engaging in behavior that would make a mother proud.
- Someone who is a creative problem solver. Sometimes a donor wants to give a restricted gift that

doesn't make sense for the organization. One of my clients had a donor who wanted to put a bench where her recently deceased husband had first kissed her. A building now stood on that site. The planned giving officer and the donor worked out the donor's ultimate goal: to commemorate the couple's time at the university where they fell in love. The planned giving officer asked, "What did you think of after he kissed you?" The donor replied, "Honeysuckle." A commemorative garden was planted, and the upkeep endowed in the donor's will. To paraphrase Humphrey Bogart's last line in *Casablanca*, "This was the beginning of a beautiful friendship."

Where to find a great major gift officer

You might want to start with your local chapter of the National Association of Charitable Gift Planners, or, if you don't have one, advertise nationally on its website. You can also advertise on the site of one of the many alphabet soups of associations. (Lots of soup here.)

You'll encounter many acronyms. Here is what these initials mean:

- JD: Attorneys have this title, which stands for Doctor of Jurisprudence (J.D., JD, D.Jr. or DJur), a three-year professional law degree. Website will be listed under American Bar Association.
- CPA: Individuals licensed as U.S. Certified Public Accountants have passed the Uniform CPA Examination. Website will be listed under AICPA.

- CFP: A Certified Financial Planner must acquire several years of experience related to delivering financial planning services to clients and pass the comprehensive CFP® Certification Exam.
- CFRE: A Certified Fund Raising Executive is an internationally recognized certification in the fundraising field and administered by CFRE International. Website will be listed under AFP, which is the Association of Fundraising Professionals.
- CLU: A Chartered Life Underwriter is a professional designation for individuals who specialize in life insurance and estate planning.

Many nonprofit management bachelor's and master's programs are sprouting up with new certifications. Also, traditional MBA programs have nonprofit management offerings.

You might want to consider hiring your first planned giving professional on a part-time basis. Many people are interested in part-time work because:

- They want to stay home with a child or an ill or elderly family member.
- They are starting a consulting practice and want an anchor client.
- They want to slow down at the end of a big-time career.
- They want to pursue another degree.
- They have a hobby or interest that they want to pursue more aggressively.

- If you offer a decent salary, flexible hours, and health insurance, you will be gobsmacked by the talent that comes out of the woodwork.

Working with volunteers

You might have interested and knowledgeable volunteers working solo or working with the planned giving staff. The volunteers could be board members or not. This is a great place for former board members who have term-limited out but know your organization and still want to be involved.

Consider my own story:

My years as a girl scout did not make for a great experience. My father took me to buy my uniform because my mother was working that day. When she arrived home, she took one look at me in my new uniform and, having emigrated from Germany in 1947, ranted at my father: "What on earth is going on, Sol? Why is Carol dressed like the Hitler Jügend? And why is she wearing a brown *yarmulke*?" My father tried to explain—unsuccessfully—to my exhausted and confused mother that he had not enrolled me in a paramilitary group.

In addition to my mother not being supportive of my girl scout experience, she was the only mother in our school who worked outside the home. Another girl had the only divorced mom. We are talking public school in the 1950s. Our scout leader, a graduate of the *Mean Girls* School of Leadership, excluded the two of us from many activities.

To this day, I remember the skills I learned in scouting: When you pick up a suitcase, bend from the knees and not the waist. When setting a table, place the knife blade facing the plate.

So, you might be wondering, why are the Girl Scouts one of the four nonprofits in my estate plan? Two words: Dianne Belk.

I went to Newport Beach, California, to present a keynote for the Girl Scouts USA on how to be more effective fundraisers. As usual, I learned more than I taught. When I heard Dianne Belk speak about planned giving to the Girl Scouts, I was fascinated. Dianne Belk is the founding chair of the Juliette Gordon Low Society Girl Scouts USA. Her husband, Lawrence Calder, is her partner in crime and volunteer extraordinaire. Their personal mission is to help knock down barriers that young women face in achieving equality. Their purpose resonated with me. The current Girl Scouts have moved past teaching girls how to pick up luggage and set a table. I was astounded by the array of learning—from nutrition to robotics—that is taking place today.

Dianne gave a simple, elegant, and powerful presentation. She told her story of becoming a girl scout. She started life as a poor Southern girl who did not have indoor plumbing until the age of 11 and lost her father a year later. But thanks to 17 scholarships she studied engineering and eventually conquered corporate America. She attributed her success to her experience with the Girl Scouts, an organization she has been involved with for 64 years. She started out very young and sold eggs to earn the dollars to belong to a troop. At the end of her speech, Dianne asked all the people who had named the Girl Scouts in their estate plans to stand. At least 15% of the audience stood. She asked them to come to the stage. She then asked anyone who planned to make a gift to come forward, and on each of them she bestowed a pin from the Juliette Gordon Low Society indicating a planned gift.

The photo op was powerful. Everyone was beaming.

Dianne spoke the next day on the specifics of planned giving. Addressing the audience, she asked, "Who thought about a planned gift last night and perhaps called a spouse or partner to discuss the possibility?" Another 11 people came forward.

I told Dianne how fabulous her speech was and gave her my card. I also wrote her a fan letter. Sure enough, when I returned to St. Louis, I got a call from her to thank me for my note and kind words. Within 15 minutes, I made a pledge for a planned gift. What made me do it?

- She asked.
- She followed up.
- She was a volunteer (she does not even let the Girl Scouts pay her expenses).
- I liked her husband. He stood behind her beaming with pride. (Lawrence looks like a cross between a

young Michael Caine and Clint Eastwood, on a day when Clint is feeling happy.)
- She invited me to dinner the next time I was in San Diego.
- She told me the name of the staff person who would be my liaison.
- She was passionate, warm, and not pushy.
- She followed through a second time and invited my husband and me to a party in San Diego. Thank you, Southwest Airlines, for your marvelous frequent flyer program. We went.

To date, Dianne has signed up more than 2,000 people as planned givers. She is a force to be reckoned with, and the future of the Girl Scouts is more secure because of her dedicated work.

Other times, the person with whom the potential donor connects is a fluke, as with Mr. L. who was in his early 90s. I asked a young man named Pete who had gone to school with my sons to join a board for which I was recruiting. I later asked him if he would mind picking up Mr. L for a 3 p.m. board meeting. Pete called me the next day to thank me. He said that, after the meeting, the older gentleman had introduced him to his favorite bar, where they had talked until after midnight. Mr. L shared stories about his days at Harvard Law School and gave business advice to the young entrepreneur. Mr. L asked Pete his thoughts on pop culture, politics, and the outing of homosexuals. Mr. L became Pete's mentor; Pete became Mr. L's chauffeur and guide to modern life. He even took the older gentleman to buy an iPhone and then taught him how to use it. When it came time for a planned giving ask, Pete was the one who went with the planned giving officer and briefed her on how to approach Mr. L. Pete told her his values and his quirks. The ask was successful.

How to find your champion or group of champions

The Girl Scouts use the term "champion," which I like, but you can be creative and think of a title that is mission-centric. For example:

- "Leader of the Pack" for an animal rescue organization
- "Goddess of Giving" for a women's organization
- "Pit Bull" for an advocacy organization with a sense of humor
- "Trailblazer" for history museums, historic trails, or reenactment groups
- "The Laird (or Lord) of the Legacy" for a Shakespearean or other theater group
- "Defender (or Guardian) of the Future" for ecology groups, children's charities, and schools
- "Evangelist" for faith-based organizations where the term is commonly used
- "Ambassador" for more formal groups

Whatever you call this person or group, here are the qualities to look for:
- People with time
- People who have already made a planned gift
- People with a passion for your mission
- People who are willing to get some training in both planned giving and speaking
- People who are professionals in your mission such as physicians, scientists, researchers, social workers, conductors (train or symphony, again depending on your mission), librarians, city planners, etc.
- People who are great at following up
- Team players who will partner with staff
- Lifelong learners

Ultimately, you need a volunteer who likes people as much as your mission. A lot of the work is connecting the mission to potential donors, which means listening to them and sharing how the work of your organization impacts lives. There are some in the nonprofit arena who value the mission over the people. You might find this ethos with animal rescue groups, arts groups, etc. If you hear someone never mentioning individuals but rather talking about the challenges facing animals or the production values of an opera company on a tight budget, this person might not be the right one for the task. The job of the champion is to connect the mission with the potential donor.

Where to recruit your ambassadors? There are any number of categories of people associated with your organization that would make great ambassadors. Remember the list of qualities and look for them amongst your:

- Board members and members of other governance structures (advisory, committee, ad hoc, honorary, etc.)
- Frontline volunteers
- Current donors
- Members of your Legacy Society, if you have one
- Former board members, former board presidents, and former longtime staff
- Alumni, former patients, or other recipients of services
- Longtime subscribers to arts organizations or sports groups
- Members if you have a membership group
- Financial advisors
- Community foundation officers
- Annual meeting audiences
- Professionals in your mission who might not be on staff

One champion is terrific. More than one is better. I am not sure what you call a group of champions. Perhaps a league, team, coalition, society, pack, coterie? I would stay away from the terms herd or coven, but the choice is yours. They should have different skills, appeal to different audiences, and take on different tasks. For instance, a financial planner or estate planning attorney might be the perfect person to speak to a peer group. For someone else, giving tours might be the hot ticket. People who are better one-on-one could accompany staff on visits or after training go on their own. Depending on your mission, you might also want to find someone with organizational, language, or travel skills who will take your potential donors on mission trips.

Training your team of champions

It is not unlike becoming a docent. Museums, zoos, and other institutions offer programs that teach their volunteer supporters to educate the public about the work that is done at their institution, whether it is distinguishing a fake Rembrandt from the real deal, examining the different types of teeth in mammals, or understanding the mechanics of a robot. It is considered an honor and a privilege to be in these programs. The same should be true of your champion program.

Your champions will learn:

- Macro and micro aspects of your organization. How many people are you serving? How many need services?
- The elements in leading a donor tour. This is very different from a tour where you are trying to impress a family with what a great educational experience

their child is going to receive. It is about what has yet to be done. It should be at least 60% listening to the potential planned giver.

- The specifics of articulating a compelling, tight, provocative, and emotionally resonant speech. It needs a clear call to action, such as asking planned givers in the audience to stand or to fill out a form on the table and hand it to the table captain, or to expect a call from someone in the organization's leadership team to set up an appointment to learn more.
- The most important facts and figures that relate to your cause. This means two to three facts, such as one in four girls and one in six boys are sexually abused by age 18, or the HLFA of Cleveland has been offering micro loans for 114 years with a repayment rate of 97%. The figures you present should be jaw-dropping.
- Guidelines to tell your own story effectively and then extrapolate so that it is relevant to your potential donors. Peter Hobler, one of the founders of Hope Happens, shared his entire family's frustration when his brother Chris was diagnosed with ALS. Not only did he share his family's story, he also revealed that every year 1 in 15 people around the world are diagnosed with a neurological disorder.
- Your champions will learn what they do best. They will discover new skills and build on old. Your champions will learn about the options for planned

giving. Bequests make up 85% to 95% of all gifts. (Various sources site different numbers, but the clear majority will leave you a specific amount or percentage.) Your champions will get an idea of what the other options might be. This learning should not be an advanced law school class but an overview.
- Your champions will not have to know everything, but they need to learn who in the organization has what knowledge so that they can steer potential planned donors to the people with the answers.
- Your champions will make friends, discover new skills, learn about your cause, and feel a sense of accomplishment.

Summary

A wide range of people are well-suited to advocating for planned gifts. These individuals can be anyone from a newly minted on-staff attorney to an 80-year old volunteer who has been leading camping trips for 50 years. You need people who are willing to learn, to listen, and to work well with others.

I WANT TO TELL YOU ABOUT
THE STRUGGLES AND DIFFICULTIES
THAT THE DISABLED HAVE TO ENDURE.

How to bring up the subject of a planned gift

How to get people engaged in talking about a charity

I was going to work with the U.S. Holocaust Museum, so I asked both residents and staff of the large building in St. Louis where I live, "When you think of the Holocaust, what comes to mind?" Here's what I heard:

- As human beings, we learned nothing. My family is from Rwanda. The genocide was in 1992. That is practically yesterday.
- Many people don't realize how many gay people were killed.
- When I teach anatomy, I always share how we learned some of the things we know and how people paid such a horrific price for this knowledge.
- I just feel sad.
- I get angry at Mel Gibson, whose father is a Holocaust-denier. I really liked his movies, but I won't go to them anymore.

I must have talked to at least 40 people. What was interesting was that not one person asked me what came to mind when I thought about the Holocaust, and some even knew my mother emigrated from Germany in 1947.

We care about what we care about. *Our job is to ask what our potential planned givers care about.*

There are many opportunities to talk about your favorite charities in a casual setting. It might be at a dinner party or a school reunion, in the grocery store, gym, or hair salon. The process is to question, ask a follow-up question, then state a fact, although not necessarily in that order. Here's an example:

You: "Do you enjoy jazz?"

Potential donor: "I love it."

You: "Who is your favorite jazz musician?"

Potential donor: "I am an old-timer. I heard Thelonious Monk in the Village in New York in the 1960s. I'll never forget it."

You: "I never heard him live. What made him so memorable?" (This is the follow-up question.)

Potential donor: "I thought he was playing for himself and not for me. It was fascinating."

You: "There is nothing like live music. Did you know there is a new nonprofit in town supporting jazz musicians, educating kids about jazz as well as producing live performances?"

Potential donor: "Tell me more."

You: "What would you like to know?"

You can easily go astray with this conversation by sharing who *your* favorite musicians are, where *you* saw them play, etc. Always get back to the donor.

The phrase "Tell me more" is an amazing gift. Don't blow it. Some folks ramble on about things like when the organization was founded, their tax status, the qualifications of the executive director, and so forth. The potential donor might have zero interest in any of these things. S(he) might want to know if there are performance opportunities or adult classes or a job for a nephew who was in the prison band. That is why the question, "What would you like to know?" is crucial.

The goal is to ask more than you tell, so that the person is engaged in the conversation rather than musing silently how to fix a wonky golf swing or what to have for dinner.

For animal shelters

Are you an animal person? Do you favor dogs or cats? I'm on the board of XYZ animal group and we have been seeing more strays. What do you think that is all about? How often do you take a walk, see someone who clearly loves his or her animal, and not stop to talk about your charity? It is the perfect opportunity. Dog parks are a fabulous place to talk about your pets and the needs of animals in your community. Everyone should be involved in your fundraising efforts, even the dogs. A retired schoolteacher asked me how she could get involved in fundraising. She was somewhat shy and had few wealthy friends. I suggested she get a doggie blanket that says, "I am in training to work with a wounded warrior. My human takes donations." The former teacher had a square for credit cards on her phone. She took in a lot of money and sent a photo and an email (as well as a tax receipt) from the dog when he was with his new human. She followed up with a photo of the new dog. The organization's donor list grew, and she and her pooch partner brought in some serious gifts.

For organizations that serve the homeless
Are you seeing more people on library steps? What do you think is going on? *Stop and listen.* I am on the board of a new homeless shelter. Would you mind if I share your thoughts or set up a meeting with the executive director? This conversation happened in the checkout line at a city library.

For arts organizations
Do you like Stravinsky? I went to the symphony last night and can't decide if I love his work or hate it. *Then listen.* Oh, I love Vivaldi too. There is going to be a Vivaldi program in the spring. Would you like to go with Frank and me?

For social service agencies
When you were a kid, did you know about opioid abuse? I was at a Family and Children's Services meeting, where

I learned that it has become an epidemic. Stop and listen. Oh, I'm so sorry your niece is having that problem as well. Would you like me to get you the name and number of someone to call at our agency to get help for her and your brother and sister-in-law?

For educational institutions
I was dumbfounded to discover how inexpensive night school is at our local university. I decided to take inorganic chemistry for fun. (My mother-in-law did this and thought it was great.) Is there something you always wanted to study? *Stop and listen.* I'm sure they have a Spanish language course. Would you like me to send a link to their website?

When you don't get the response, you want

If the person you are talking with says:
- I am allergic to animals and can't stand being around them.
- The homeless are just lazy and should be shipped to Siberia.
- Opioid abuse, drinking and promiscuity, drinking, and drugs are just three of the many reasons I don't have children.
- Why would I want to pay to go to a university at night when I can watch the new season of *Orange is the New Black*?

Let it go.

Some of us like to dance, some of us would rather canoe than hear a lecture, and some people, Jimmy Carter being a prime example, would rather build a house than sit in a board meeting. Your job is to find out if your organization might be a fit for an initial "date."

How to bring up the subject of planned giving, or let's talk about your death

Planned giving can be a touchy topic. I remember bringing it up in a board retreat in Atlanta, where a middle-aged guy told me I had no business discussing what people put in their wills.

"Why?" I asked.

He said, "That is just none of your damn business."

He was about 6'5" and had played semi-pro football. I am 5'1" and used to play a little high school tennis. I let the subject drop. It was the strongest reaction I have ever had, but I am sure that many people think the way he does. That might be one of the reasons so many Americans do not have an estate plan. According to a 2015 Rocket Lawyer estate-planning survey by Harris Poll, 64% of Americans don't have a will. Of those without a plan, about 27% said they didn't feel an urgent need for one and 15% said they didn't need one at all. It's partially because most people, especially the young, think that they are immortal, and partially because they falsely believe wills are only for those with multimillion-dollar estates.

The word "estate" is interesting. For many people, it conjures up an extraordinary property like Southfork Ranch on the old TV show "Dallas" or Downton Abbey in the PBS series. But where planned giving is concerned, these images are misleading. An $80,000 house and a $50,000 life insurance policy also make a good-sized estate. For those of you who live in high real estate priced markets such as San Francisco, Austin, or New York City, in the Midwest we have houses that are quite nice that cost less than the Gross Domestic Product of a small country.

When to ask

People are most willing to discuss the subject when a major change has occurred in their lives. This change can be perceived as either good or bad. Don't make a premature judgment. I once had a friend over for dinner the day her divorce became final. One of the other guests said, "This must be a very difficult time for you." My friend said, "This is the happiest day of my life. The worst day of my life was when I found out my husband wasn't working at Best Buy and was selling drugs!" There have been times when I have said to a close friend whose parent died after years of dementia, "Thank goodness it is over." Obviously, you would never say this to someone whose circumstances were not well known to you.

Here are some times when people might be willing to talk about estate planning:

- Marriage
- Divorce
- Birth of a child
- Death of a child
- Adoption
- Sale of a company
- Retirement
- Death of a spouse
- Death of a parent
- Inheritance from a relative
- Inheritance from a non-relative
- Large payday from the sale of a company. This can be a company owned by the beneficiary or a company that was bought out, such as Anheuser-Busch, which, when sold to InBev, paid off stockholders.
- Diagnosis of an illness in oneself or spouse
- A birthday approaching the age when a parent died
- Purchase of a house or land
- An international trip where a couple with minor children are traveling together without the children

Getting the appointment

When you feel it might be a good time to ask, an introduction from a friend, colleague, or family member of the potential donor can fling doors wide open. Many board members don't feel comfortable asking friends, often because of the quid pro quo. You give to my cause; therefore, I must give to yours. Board members need to be assured that making the introduction is all that they need to do.

Do you write, call, email, or visit? The answer is often at least three modes of communication. More and more, introductions are through email. Here's an example:

Dear Jamie and Scott,

I really want you to meet each other. Scott, Jamie is the gift officer I told you about who works for our alma mater. He helped me figure out how to give more money and pay less taxes. I'm afraid he is a Cubs fan, but no one is perfect. I gave Jamie your cell number, so expect his call.

All the best,
Larry (aka your board member)

Other times, a letter of introduction from the development professional is the hot ticket. Something like:

Dear Dr. Chang and Dr. Pittman,

Since I joined the Arthritis Foundation, your names have come up many times. The staff shared with me your interest in research as well as your generosity.

I recently moved here from Omaha, where I worked for the American Cancer Society, so I am new to the issues facing people with arthritis. I have been reading everything I can get my hands on and would appreciate a meeting to learn more about your ongoing research interests. I will call in the next week to hopefully set up a time for a visit.

Sincerely,
Karyn Buxman, MPH, RN
Major Gift Officer

Or, the letter can come from the executive director. It would read something like this:

Dear Wes and Mary Ann,

We have a new major gift officer I would like you to meet. She has master's degrees in both public health and nursing. Karyn went into development five years ago in Omaha. Her husband just landed a job as the concertmaster for the symphony, so they have relocated here. All her experience is with the American Cancer Society. I would appreciate it if you would share with her your experiences with the research you have funded and your thoughts on the pace of progress with rheumatoid arthritis.

Her name is Karyn Buxman. I will have her reach out to you in the next few days.

All the best,
Pete Noback
Executive Director

P.S. Thank you for suggesting that I take my wife to that Italian restaurant for our anniversary dinner. It was spectacular!

What happens when your calls, emails, and letters are not answered? Three choices:
- Have a pity party and talk about how rude people are
- Take them off your list
- Get creative

If you start with number three, here are a few things you might try. First, work your six degrees of separation magic. Always start with your board and staff. If they don't know your prospect, hit the web. Use LinkedIn to see if you know any of the same people to facilitate an introduction. Google their names. Maybe they have left town or been indicted.

If you know that the address is correct, send a box of mixed nuts with a card that says, "All the sixth graders at our school are nuts about the centrifuge you purchased for our science center. Would you like to set up a time to come visit our school or for me to visit you to share how the children are using it? The creativity of the sixth-grade student is mind-boggling."

Or, you might send a big box of lifesavers with the note, "Thanks to you, parents of children with severe autism are getting respite care. You have made it possible for parents to enjoy a night out on an anniversary, celebrate another child's birthday, or just relish some alone time. You really are a lifesaver. Might there be a time when I could come by and share what your donation has meant to our families, or, if more convenient, when you could visit our residential home? I am not sure I have your correct phone number. Would you please call me at your convenience at 314-562-3350?

Again, many thanks for your generosity. You have changed lives."

You can get Lifesaver candies with your logo and contact information on the packaging.

Ultimately, your time is valuable, and it might just be time to say, "Next." We really don't know what is going on in other people's lives. There could be a divorce stewing, a new grandchild on the way, or an unexpected setback. You might have to live without ever knowing. Just realize that the reason probably has nothing to do with you and move on. If this is someone you have already met and you didn't click, consider turning the potential donor over to another staff or board person. None of us like everyone and you could be the spitting image of a former spouse.

A pity party is fine, as long as you keep it short and sweet. Remember, your goal is not everyone else's problem.

How to talk about a planned gift

Simple words always trump formal words. Use the words your potential donor uses. If she says it is a joy to finally meet you, you are going to talk about the joy of knowing that the work she is now supporting will continue. Once you move past a simple bequest, you are in major alphabet soup area. When you see your donor's eyes glaze over, you know you are in trouble.

Try to talk about outcome rather than product. For instance, you might ask the donor if s(he) would like a life income rather than discuss the specific process involved. Or perhaps your potential donor needs or wants a current tax deduction. This desire is particularly common after selling a company.

Dr. Russell James suggests using the phrase: "gifts that pay you income and avoid taxes." Other appealing terms to discuss gifts: "Easier, smarter, simpler."

Some words will resonate with your potential donors more than others. You might want to use words like "giving" rather than "philanthropy," especially with middle-class donors. Religious groups have their own language referring to the act of giving. The more you know and understand the language of your donor, the better.

Speak conversationally, warmly, and respectfully, as though you were speaking to a favorite aunt, uncle, or former teacher. There's a movement in many fields to simplify jargon. In many hospitals, you are treated by a cancer, kidney, or lung doctor rather than by an oncologist, nephrologist, or pulmonologist.

The simpler the concept and language, the more relaxed the person and the easier the decision. Technical questions can always be addressed, but they should be the technical questions of the donor. Before deciding about major or planned giving, a solar engineer might ask whether a project will be LEED Platinum, a teacher might wonder about the methodology used and testing conducted, an accountant might want to look at your audit. I am a social worker by training, so if a meeting becomes too technical I bring my financial advisor.

I always ask women as well as men if they would like to bring anyone else along. Some of my colleagues believe that when discussing a gift, it is demeaning to ask a woman if she would like to bring a friend or relative to the conversation. I understand where they are coming from. Decades ago, when my husband was stationed at Fort Bragg, we needed a minivan, so I was at a dealership looking at cars. The salesman asked when my husband would be available. I told him that I was purchasing the car. He said, "Well, it is his money," at

CONCLUDING WITH, "LET'S ALL STAND AND APPLAUD," IS NOT WHAT WE MEANT BY "A CALL TO ACTION."

which point I asked to speak to the manager. The good news is that I wasn't armed!

I think we have evolved since that day, and the car salesman is either unemployed or has caught on that women make both money and decisions. I disagree that it is rude to ask if a man or woman contemplating a large financial decision would like to bring someone to the discussion. The smartest people I know ask other smart people for advice. The highest compliment I have ever been paid was by my nephew Jake, then age 10:

"What I admire most about you, Aunt Carol, is that all of your friends are smarter than you."

"If you are the smartest person in the room," I said, "find another room. You will learn more."

"But what if you are in prison?" he asked.

The discussion devolved from there.

As part of your donor research, if a board member or volunteer knows your prospect, ask which phrases will resonate with their friend or colleague:
- Make a philanthropic investment
- Make a transfer of assets
- Give money to charity and not to the government
- Make a gift
- Make a bequest
- Leave a legacy

If you can't get that information before your meeting, you can simply ask people: How do you see yourself when it comes to giving money to charity?

What are you looking for in a donation, or what is your philosophy of giving? Personally, I give planned gifts to organizations if I have either served on the board, have great respect for their leadership, or have used or enjoyed their services. (One rarely enjoys a hospital, but a theater is another matter). Don't assume others have the same philosophy as you do. Some are wildly different.

One man shared his philosophy: "I give where I have failed or where I have not been able to contribute the way that I wanted. I was set to go into the Peace Corp when my mother was diagnosed with cancer. I got a job, stayed home, and took care of her. I have never regretted the time I spent with her. I got married. We had kids. I wanted to work in East Africa but never did. I wanted to do more for my high school friend who became an alcoholic and died while driving drunk. My choices and dreams do not have to die with me. I have arthritis and traversing O'Hare Airport without a wheelchair is starting to feel like crossing the Sahara wearing flip-flops. And I really hate using a wheelchair, but I am ultimately a realist. Through my legacy gift to a school in Rwanda, I can empty my very full bucket list. So far, I have sponsored nine young leaders to work in the school. They come home and tell me heartwarming as well as heartbreaking stories. These trips will go on long after I am gone. I would make the same decisions all over again and feel good about them, but ultimately life is very, very short."

I love his philosophy that his dreams do not have to die with him.

Here are some phrases that will help you frame your request:

- "I give to charities with a long track record. If they have been in business at least 50 years, they are doing something right. They are dependable, so when I die, hopefully not for another 50 years, they will still be in business. Health causes are the only exception. I want heart disease, cancer, and other diseases cured before I go."
  - In this case, frame your ask in terms of the longevity and reliability of your charity: *As a 73-year-old non-profit, we pride ourselves on our long record of service, and with your vision and generosity it will continue.*
- "I look for money well spent. If a charity spends more than ten percent on overhead, they can go elsewhere. They are not for me."
  - Your response will be: *We have always been client-focused both in how we spend our time and your money. With your help, we can continue to deliver great services with our current 9% margin.*
- "I look to innovation when making decisions. I want to see cutting-edge work. People who are risk-averse are not my kind of people. I want to give to organizations that aren't afraid to make mistakes and learn from them. As an entrepreneur, I've learned more from my failures than from my successes."

- You pick up on this theme with: *We have always been at the forefront of trying new techniques and practices. And you are correct, we don't exactly celebrate our failures, but we always make sure we learn from them and adjust course.*
- "I look where my peers are giving. If they are on the board and know the organization inside and out, then I am interested in finding out more."
  - Your reply: *I know you are friends with Marianne and Mike Murphy. They became board members and legacy society donors along with Gina Fusco, and no one is smarter when it comes to charitable investing than those three.*

Listen to the differences in the following phrases:
- I think you have a great program.
- I feel you have a great program.
- I feel passionate about our cause. (It is important to note when a prospective major or planned giver uses the term "our," you can do the happy dance, if only in your head.)
- I love our work with the food bank.
- I appreciate the blessing in our mission.
- I know in my heart that God has put me on this earth to be a part of this work.

You need to respond using *their* language. If they use the word "love" that is the word you need to repeat. You might say, "I love the progress we've made since we have enough funds for more staff." Or, you could mention to the person who is peer-conscious whom he might know on your board. If your donor uses the term "mature organization," you can begin sentences with "As a mature organization..."

It takes a while to really listen to the donor's words. Sometimes you can't mirror the language if you are not familiar or comfortable with it. For instance, if your donor speaks about Jesus as our Lord and Savior and you are not a Christian, using religious language will come off as awkward and insincere. The biggest challenge is that frequently we are thinking more about how we are going to respond to someone's words than listening carefully to them. The less you concentrate on your next sentence, the better you can hear the potential donor's priorities.

A surgeon I was training in fundraising said that she found it very difficult to have conversations about money. So I asked her:

"When did you have your last 'Do not resuscitate' conversation?"

"This morning."

"How did you learn to have compassionate conversations about such heartrending decisions?"

"I had a marvelous mentor."

"What's the difference," I asked, "between your approach today and your approach when you first started practicing?"

"Today I focus on the patient and the family and not on what I'm going to say next."

"That's the same approach to use in conversations about giving. And the more you do it, the easier it will be to focus on the needs and wants of the donor."

"I can't imagine asking someone for $100,000 or more."

"It can be as wonderful as telling someone they are cancer-free. The $100,000 will bring joy to the donor and one day a cure for cancer."

She mused, "It will take more than $100,000 to cure cancer."

"Then ask for more. When I started fundraising," I went on, "I would play the theme song from the movie *Rocky* on my way to visit a donor."

"The *Flight of the Valkyries* is more my style."

"Go with that then. Whatever helps you feel confident. The biggest difference between medical and fundraising conversations is that when you give a patient the news of a diagnosis with a poor prognosis and only surgery, chemo, radiation, or hospice in their future, they will have a very bad day. When you give people an opportunity to make their dreams and visions for the future come true, they are filled with hope and joy."

Six months later, I heard from the director of advancement that this doc was asking patients, "Would you like to partner with me on a cure? I'll put in the long hours and brainpower if you will join me in funding the work."

She was also teaching her residents and interns to say the same thing. You hear amazing stories when you really listen. I once did a board retreat for a formal music group that performed in a large, gilded hall. I asked the board members, "Has there been a time in your life when music really spoke to you?" A buttoned-up mathematician said, "I would like to start." He looked tight as a tic. Thinking his comments would be boring, if not grim, I groaned inwardly.

"Many years ago, I was doing a post-doc in Vienna," he said. "I was having coffee and strudel in a plaza. The sun was shining, and there was a string quartet playing. I looked over and saw the most interesting-looking woman I had ever seen sitting alone, swaying to the music and reading a book. I am a shy guy. The music gave me the courage to walk over and ask if I could join her. We will be married 29 years in May."

The entire board was flabbergasted. They had never taken this gentleman as a romantic. Other board members then shared their stories—times when music helped them to heal, to grieve, or to celebrate. They were used to talking about music as an art form either to preserve the classics or to educate the young. For the first time, they talked about music in terms of its effect on people's lives. They began to see that asking for continued funding was a way to help people live fuller, happier lives. Their discussion that morning gave them another framework in which to ask their friends, colleagues, and peers to join them in a planned gift.

Death is a difficult subject. The person whose end is imminent might be willing to talk and, in fact, might need to, but loved ones might not be prepared. I remember when my two sisters and I divided up my mother's jewelry. Mom thought it was prudent to make decisions while she was still alive and was perfectly comfortable with the idea. She suffered from emphysema (three packs a day of unfiltered Camels will do that. She had a figure like Jane Fonda and the lungs of an ancient coal miner. She had already been near death several times. We cut cards to see who would start first. It all went well until one of my sisters lost it and started sobbing. The thought of our mother being gone was just too much for her.

When Frank and I wrote our will, we insisted that our grown sons go with us to the attorney's office. They didn't want to go. When our son Jono was in 11th grade, he gave us for Christmas funeral urns that he'd made in ceramics class. When it came to squeamishness about our ultimate demise I told him that he didn't have a leg to stand on. We asked our sons if they wanted to be joint executors, and the younger said he wanted nothing to do with it and our older son could do it. When we said that the executor might get paid, our younger son said that he didn't care—he didn't want to deal with the business end of it. We also discussed our charitable contributions. Our son the art teacher called the next day and said that he thought we had made a mistake with a planned gift to the school where he taught. He asked if we had stipulated the art department. We hadn't, so I went back to the lawyer and changed the language. Each son has a copy of the will.

Our sons don't know how much will be in the estate at the time of our deaths. We feel frisky, but who knows? Could be a lot, could be a little. But our sons understand what we value. We also think it is important to understand what our children value, so we are giving to what *they* think is important. The ceramics program at a specific high school would not be in our estate plan except that our son loves the school, the work, and the students. We are also giving to a medical program where my mother worked and my daughter-in-law sought care to honor what they value.

Many people don't want to share their estate-planning decisions with their children or other heirs. Some people wield their will as a sword over the heads of children and charities. The message is that if you don't do things my way, you will not inherit. According to my mentor Jerry Horwitz, "The biggest mistake a person can make is to try to control beyond the grave. Be careful, be prudent, and enjoy today."

We wanted to explain our thinking on why we had planned as we had. If we both die at the same time, each son gets 40% of the estate; 10% goes to charities; and 10% goes to nieces, nephews, and friends who have helped us in our lives. Our financial advisor, John Russell, has been such a wonderful friend that he gets $1,000 for a dinner and Broadway show in New York.

(This was pre-*Hamilton* when you could bring a friend, see a show, and have dinner without taking a second mortgage. We may have to rethink this.) We shared with our sons all that he had done for us.

Most people don't want to think about death. And thinking about the age of a death is relative. My mother called to tell me that a friend of hers had died and he was only 82. I said, "Mom, he was a man, not a tree." My perception of death was colored by years of working as a medical social worker in pediatric oncology in the 1970s. The death rate from cancer for children from infancy to 18 was very different from today. The age of 82 sounded ancient. But then, I was 24 and had seen many children under ten succumb to cancer.

You and your donors' lives are influenced by the experience of the death of a loved one or a peer. Also, the age at which a parent of the same sex dies is relevant. My husband's grandfather died at 52. Frank's dad was amazed when he hit 53. He lived into his late 80s. Some people will talk very comfortably about the end of their lives and others find it acutely uncomfortable. When you encounter people who are clearly uncomfortable, ask them if they mind sharing the reason for their discomfort. I have heard answers such as, "I still have a very big bucket list." Or, "I was not the parent I should have been, and my children are making bad choices."

At a high school reunion, an old friend said, "My brothers and I were dealt all aces and we still managed to lose." My next question was based on Sam's philosophy of "It's not over until it's over." I asked her what she would like as a "do-over." She said she wanted to be a jock again. Later I ran into her and she said that she hired a personal trainer. Her eloquent quote on transforming into the athlete she once was: "This guy is kicking my butt and I am loving getting into shape."

One conversation that broke my heart was with a man who had ALS. He had watched his grandfather and cousin die of this cruelly debilitating disease. He said, "I don't want my kids to have to wipe my bottom or spoon-feed me. Fortunately, I have the money to hire staff, but the whole process of slowly not being able to take care of myself makes me angry and frustrated." We used this as a starting point to discuss why a cure was so important. "This disease doesn't just steal your life," he said. "It steals your dignity."

We talked at length about how to preserve the dignity of people living with ALS and how to help them until there is a cure. He felt good about his planned gift, which would provide funding for ALS research, as well as home health care for those with the illness. He felt that this gift was one of the few things he could do to make his inevitable decline easier for others.

Going into the military or other high-risk professions puts mortality on the table. When my husband went active duty in the Army, he had to have a will. A JAG officer wrote it in less than ten minutes. It covered the basics and perhaps would not pass muster with most sophisticated attorneys, but it was done, and it was free. If you are married to a police officer, firefighter, race car driver, a member of a bomb squad, or a performer with Cirque de Soleil, there would be little question that a will is a good idea. This might not be an easy discussion if a risk-taking spouse takes pride in tempting fate.

The decision-making process

The idea of a planned gift frequently starts with the magic phrase or thought: I wish I could do more.

Elizabeth Kübler-Ross describes the five stages of grief in her book *On Death and Dying*. Helping people make decisions *before* they are ill can involve almost as much work, and sometimes even more, than when they *are* dying. Here are some guidelines when approaching healthy donors:

- Most of the time, when you are approaching a person who is not ill, a significant question you must deal with is: Why now? I have discussed some of the reasons donors decide the time is right, such as divorce, inheritance, international travel without their children, the sale of a company, etc. As mentioned before, the most difficult issues that donors must grapple with frequently involve their children. How much is too much? What is fair? The list goes on. Childless folks are much freer to make generous charitable decisions. Whether someone has children is a delicate subject. Some people never wanted children, some couldn't have children, and some had children who died. You need to know if your perspective donor is a parent. Tread delicately.

- If you are working with a family struggling with a difficult situation, you might have some creative ideas of your own. One of my friends had a 26-year-old with a drug problem. The mother had worked hard all her life. Her husband had died two years before she sat down to rewrite her estate plan. Her two other children were doing well, both working, one married with a child. Her lawyer suggested that the son with the drug habit be given 1/10 of his share yearly if he passed three months of random drug testing. Every year that he flunked meant the money remained in the fund. At the end of ten years, if he had passed all the drug tests, he would receive a bonus. Every time that he was clean, and only then, would he get the funds. At the end of the ten years, any money that had remained in the fund would go to a choral group that had supported the mother during her son's three stints in rehab. Instructions to her first and back-up trustees were very clear. She was a bit compulsive, so she put the instructions in writing, discussed them in person with the trustees, and then videotaped them in case the trustees predeceased her. Once she realized how much her choral group had supported her during the death of her husband and the addiction of her son, she also gave an immediate gift to them.

- Avoid the phrase, "You might get hit by a car tomorrow." I remember a life insurance salesman asking me in a very melodramatic voice, "What will happen to you if Frank doesn't come home one day?" I said, in an equally melodramatic voice: "I will beep him." All in all, we were very annoyed with this guy. We were in our 20s, and the salesman had not approached the subject in a way we could hear. He hadn't considered that Frank was a medical student facing death every day and frequently feeling helpless. He hadn't considered that I was the breadwinner making the princely (or in my case, princess-ly) sum of $9,500 a year. The salesman addressed all his questions to Frank. I wanted to say, "Buddy, it might be his life, but it is *my* money that is going to pay the premiums." He never asked if I should have life insurance. I guess he assumed that I could be replaced in a matter of weeks, which might have been true...but still.

- When talking about planned giving, look for the positive outcomes for the donor. Talk about what the donor values, what has been helpful and positive in his or her life. If the donor continues to talk about how unnecessary an estate plan is at this age, ask if s(he) has known anyone who has passed away younger than they are today. I have never heard a "No." This question usually helps you move forward.

- Many parents are in the fortunate position of being able to help their children buy a first house. The parents might consider a condition of the gift that the child make a will. The adult children might believe they are invincible, but the money that Mom and Dad shelled out is real.

- Your donor who is ill might have a very real death-related motivation. Allow your donor to talk and listen carefully. Ask questions like:
  - What are you most proud of?
  - What is the smartest decision you have ever made?
  - Who was the most influential person in your life?
  - What is the best gift you have ever received?
  - What is the best gift you have ever given?
  - Is there something on your bucket list that is still nagging at you?

The answers will give you the clues to motivate giving. Caveat: The gift might not go to your organization. In one story I heard, a gift officer asked a friend's grandfather about his greatest regret. The grandfather answered, "I always wanted to hike the Appalachian Trail." The gift officer asked if he could share this thought with the man's family. He said yes. One son and three grandsons said they would hike the trail in his honor and would create a book commemorating not only the journey but also the man's life. It would be a legacy for the whole family, as well as for the children yet to be born. The grandfather was so thrilled with the idea that he earmarked money for the trip. That meant the charity got a little less, but the family was grateful. You know that the planned giving officer was going to follow up with the family when they took their hike!

- Some people need to plan to plan. What is important are the goal-setting and the timing. One friend I asked about a planned gift said that she wanted her entire family to discuss it together. This conversation took place the week before Valentine's Day. I asked when her family was getting together, and she said, "Thanksgiving." We talked about what to email and share with her family on the organizations she wanted to support (especially the one whose board I served on), as well as to reassure that there was plenty loot for all of them. When Thanksgiving came around, she set aside time after dinner to talk to her children and older grandchildren. She also had set up an appointment the next day with her attorney, who was gracious enough to come over and talk with everyone. She didn't have a medical power of attorney and many other instruments in place, but by the time the attorney left the entire family felt that there was a solid plan.

- Share permanent opportunities, such as a wall of legacy donors or membership in legacy societies. Many of us want recognition in our lifetime and want to share what we value. There is nothing wrong with wanting to name a yacht, but when it is sold the name will immediately change. Naming a program, classroom, building, or scholarship might bring more lasting joy.

Exception to the rule: Some nonprofits are founded because of a planned gift, so the process is reversed. The money appears and then the infrastructure is built.

Summary

When talking about planned giving, be mindful that you are talking about what will happen after your donor dies. People have different reactions to this topic. Some are excited about the possibilities, some are queasy, and others shut down altogether. Take it slow, and above all, listen. Ask questions. Then listen some more.

...A THOUGHTFUL GIFT THAT REFLECTS YOUR PROSPECT'S INTERESTS.

8

How to steward your donors

What is stewardship?

Businesses call it "relationship management."
Mothers call it "minding your manners."

Stewardship is the art and science of making sure that the people who give to your organization feel appreciated and want to stay involved.

Basic Principles

- Are you thanking once? Twice? At all?
- Expressing gratitude is a marvelous way for board members who hate to ask to be engaged in the fundraising process. This is also true for people who are either prohibited by law from fundraising, like judges, or by circumstances such as being an executive director of another nonprofit. The more personal the thank you, the greater the chances for a second and larger gift. There is an old axiom:

"Find seven ways to thank your donors and they will quickly give again."

- The more meaningful the thank you, the greater the chances for a second and larger gift.
- Always try to make a thank-you gift both creative and low-cost.
- Some people prefer not to be publicly acknowledged. Respect their wishes.
- Treat every legacy donor as if the gift were revocable, even if it is irrevocable. What this means is that even if the donor cannot change the estate gift (an irrevocable gift), you need to be just as attentive as though the gift were revocable (meaning the estate plan can be changed).

Planned givers who are well-stewarded are more likely to encourage others, to share the information with friends and family, and to give additional funds.

If you have a physical site that has a lot of foot traffic, naming opportunities are always a possibility. This is particularly true for arts venues, educational facilities, and hospitals. The most important aspect of naming rights is that they should never be in perpetuity. Perpetuity is a very, very long time. I'll talk more about this later.

There are basically two types of stewardship for individual donors: specific acts of kindness and highly recognizable symbols. The first kind of stewardship is more labor-intensive, takes more creativity, and is fabulous for large donors. With large groups of planned givers, a recognizable pin can frequently do the trick. I am almost 70 and don't wear T-shirts, don't carry tote bags, and don't want another umbrella. A small unisex pin works for many people. It is sort of like the Oscar statue. The gold guy doesn't stand one year and sit the next—he is always the same. That is because winners want something that is immediately recognizable. The reason I prefer a pin to a statue is that when you are attending a social event, it is difficult to carry a drink, a purse, and a statue. The advantage to bowls, trophies, and statues is that they stand out in an office. However, with more of your planned givers working at home, retired, or downsizing, unless it is a truly marvelous sculpture or statue, forget it. Think about what works best for your donors.

I had a client who wanted to give a large picture of children's handprints to a generous family that supported a child abuse program. They were serious art collectors and told me that they had only their very favorite works displayed and that two-thirds of their collection was in storage. I suggested the organization ask the entire family to the Christmas party for the children in the special preschool. The planned giver said that he would be Santa Claus if they wanted, that he had his own Santa suit.

You can give artwork if you really know the person's tastes or if the art is a joke. One of my clients, another serious art collector, guffawed at the painting of Elvis on velvet that a fellow board member had picked up by the side of the road on a trip to Texas. The donor hung it in his office and laughed every time he shared the story with his visitors.

Do not go by the golden rule. It is all about the platinum rule, as spelled out by Dr. Tony Alessandra. The golden rule is to treat others as we want to be treated; the platinum rule is to treat others as *they want to be treated. You might love a big party to celebrate a gift. Others might prefer an intimate dinner or a provocative lecture or a mission trip. Know your donor.*

Stewardship done well

Let's start with big league, individual stewardship. My dear friend and former boss, Dr. Arthur Prensky, was an unlikely child to grow up to be a planned giver. He was born in New York 88 years ago to a mentally ill mother and a father who was a part-time taxi driver and illegal bookmaker. His parents were divorced when he was young. When his mother was suicidal, Arthur, then age 10, would sleep in Central Park.

Arthur had one thing going for him: He was brilliant. Arthur was accepted into Bronx Science High, which is a free school for gifted students. Among its graduates are seven Nobel Prize winners and many other luminaries, including Arthur, whose resume includes college at Cornell, medical school at New York University, and residency at Harvard. He went on to chair the pediatric neurology department at St. Louis Children's Hospital and received the first named professorship in pediatric neurology in the U.S.

He made his first planned gift to Washington University while his first wife, Sheila, was still alive. They had no children, and they had both worked at the university and were loyal to it.

Arthur and Sheila decided on a visiting professorship. The medical school assumed it would be getting the money. Both Arthur and Sheila were art lovers and ran a lithograph company on the side.

When they approached the University's art school about endowing a visiting scholar program, a staff member visited the couple in their home. Arthur was incredibly touched that someone would drive 35 minutes to their house. I told him that, considering the amount of money involved, he could have asked them to meet him for lunch in Thailand.

Arthur wanted a life income, which was set up as an annuity. Sheila passed away, and later when he was 80, he married Vivian, whom he met on the dating site eHarmony. (I wrote his profile!) He called when he married Vivian to tell me that the art school had sent them an orchid. He was touched. It was the only wedding present he ever mentioned to me. Since that time, he regularly establishes gift annuities to both the art and medical schools.

Stewardship done badly

After a board retreat I facilitated on the East Coast, I sat next to a wealthy board member at dinner. I asked him what was the most rewarding gift he had ever received, and he said that he would gladly tell me the worst. He had endowed a chair at a university (so we are talking $1.5 million and up, depending on the institution), and as a thank you, the gift officer invited him and his wife to a baseball game. Being from South America, his game was football, not baseball. He made sure I knew that it was the real football, in other words, soccer. His wife was a victim of post-polio syndrome and, at the time, was in a wheelchair recovering from orthopedic surgery. She was sitting across the table and said that regardless of her orthopedic status, she too didn't like baseball. Her husband said that the only way he would ever go to a baseball game was if he was seated next to a head of state, preferably President Clinton. This surprised me, since I assumed that the donor was a Republican. "Why Clinton?" I asked. He said he wanted to find out if he was as charming as everyone said, and wanted to ask his advice about women. When his wife heard this comment, she shook her finger at him.

I asked what would have been a better way for the university to thank him. He said that he would have preferred dinner with all of the Ph.D. candidates in the program he funded to hear their thoughts on the future of the field. Had I known the gift officer, I would have called him. Instead, I suggested that the philanthropist call the chairman of the department and ask for such a meeting. The donor and his wife became very excited. The wife looked at her husband and said, "Remember how hungry we were when you were a student and I was pregnant? Let's have a large basket of food for each of them to take home." They started to talk about what day to have the Ph.D. candidates for dinner, what food to serve for the meal, and what to put in the baskets. The couple said that they didn't want any departmental professors, only the doctoral students. They thanked me profusely for the idea, which had been theirs.

Another example of great stewardship

Every Sunday morning, Stanley Lopata came to visit my mother. He drove up in his vintage Rolls Royce and came to the door with a bag of bagels. My children knew him as "The Bagel Man." Years before, he started visiting a housebound friend on Sunday mornings, bringing bagels and staying for a cup of coffee. After the death of his friend, the tradition continued, and the route expanded. I didn't know until I got engaged, but Stanley also had an ice bucket with Champagne in his Rolls Royce in case there was something to celebrate.

One Sunday morning, we were at Mom's and Stanley strutted in wearing a Washington University letter jacket. Stanley was a poor kid who didn't get to play a sport when he was a student at Washington University in St. Louis. He studied chemical engineering, became an inventor, and, with his German wife Lucy's gift of her war reparation money, founded the Carboline Corporation. With Stanley's genius and Lucy's support, they made mega bucks. Not only was Stanley incredibly successful, he was also exceedingly generous. In addition to giving his time as a board member and financing numerous buildings on campus, he endowed a basketball tournament called "The Lopata Classic." The development staff at Washington University did two brilliant things to say thank you:

- All the players from both teams came onto the court wearing bow ties, Stanley's signature apparel. After the national anthem, the ties came off and the game began.
- They gave him a letter jacket.

Stanley strolled in and asked my sons, then ages seven and nine, what they thought about his jacket. One said, "I don't like the color." The other said, "It doesn't cover your butt. You are going to get cold." Stanley said, "This is the best present I have ever received in my life." And he meant it.

When you have a dedicated donor or board member who is extremely rich, and you can't imagine what to do to demonstrate your gratitude, how do you proceed? Here are a few rules of thumb so that your stewardship is done well:

- Ask a family member or friend if there is an experience your donor has always wanted. Sky diving? Seeing a rehearsal of Alvin Alley's dance company? (This is my secret wish.) Throwing out a ball at a pro game? What does your donor want that you could make happen?

HOW TO STEWARD YOUR DONORS · 179

- Ask if there is anyone your donor has always wanted to meet. I wrote my husband's favorite poet, Dorothy Porter, in Australia and asked if she and her partner would have dinner with Frank and me for his 50th birthday. I almost pulled it off, but at the last minute she had to be in Sydney during the time I was working in Melbourne.
- Does your donor have a favorite author? Can you get a signed copy of the book with a note from the author? Obviously, if the favorite book is the Bible, *The Canterbury Tales*, or *The Adventures of Huckleberry Finn*, you are out of luck. But there might be a contemporary writer your donor admires. If you can work your six degrees of separation magic, you might even get a video clip from the author.
- Have the best-known person in your sphere of influence call. I'm thinking someone like Colin Powell or Tom Hanks or Michelle Obama. If you don't know any of these folks (I don't), do the best you can. I had a very nice email exchange with Dr. Sanjay Gupta, a neurosurgeon who's the chief medical correspondent for CNN. At the end of the note asking for a 10-minute interview about getting him involved with a board for which I was recruiting, I told him how much I enjoyed his book, *Monday Mornings*. He emailed back in 45 minutes. It didn't work out for him to get involved with the board. It turns out that working as an on-air journalist, practicing neurosurgery, and having a family takes a lot

of time. Who knew? But I did hear from him. As we all know, if you don't ask, you don't get.

- Is there something symbolic of your mission that you could give? We gave machetes to board members of the "Friends of the Eternal Rainforest" who traveled to field stations in Costa Rica on a major donor mission trip. When we returned, we gave each participant a machete with a luggage tag with the donor's name on one side and "Defender of the Forest" on the other. One of the guys who works in our building lugged the case of machetes up to my office. When he asked what was in the heavy box and I said a case of machetes, he asked why. I told him, "Marital problems." Luckily, he didn't believe me. Considering the funds raised, the machetes were inexpensive—and memorable.

Some guidelines:

- Give gifts that are inexpensive and carefully chosen.
- If your donor is shy or wants to remain anonymous, give the gift in private.
- If your donor enjoys recognition, give it in front of the people s(he) cares about. Think family, religious leader, colleagues, and peers.
- Experiential gifts that relate to the mission or to your donor's passion are frequently the hot ticket.
- Consider a custom video or book that shows the impact of the gift.

Always remember: Special people deserve special recognition. Get your most creative, Pinterest-reading, glue-gun-toting, Martha Stewart-types involved.

Mixed reviews

I work with a retreat center that has had mixed results with their stewardship program. The center has a religious heritage but is open to all. I started calling legacy donors who had named this organization in their will. I asked if they thought they had been appropriately stewarded. About half said yes and half said no.

Here are some of the responses I heard after asking, "Do you feel appreciated?"

- "My name was read aloud at a meeting. I never gave anyone permission to share this information. I was appalled and embarrassed. My adult kids were upset with me. They said the money should be going to their children's education." (Remember, philanthropy can be perceived as the enemy of inheritance).
- "We were asked for a large gift for the capital campaign. We didn't have the amount asked for, but we said we would make a planned gift. The person asking was so visibly disappointed that we feared we'd be murdered in our beds so that the retreat center would get the money sooner. Fortunately, the person asking was not violent."
- "We got a pin that was a church. I thought it was a lovely way to recognize our gift."

- "We got a pin that was a church. We don't belong to a church and would never wear something like that."
- "There was a party for everyone who had made a planned gift and we were all given a bottle of Champagne. I have been in recovery for 16 years. Everyone knows this. What knucklehead thought a gift of booze was a good idea?"
- "I thought the Champagne party was lovely. I got to see my friends. It was held late afternoon, which was considerate for people like me who don't drive at night."

Successful stewardship is not easy. We decided to do an online survey of all the people who attended the retreat center. It went something like this:

This survey is anonymous unless you choose to share your name. We want to do a better job of thanking people in a meaningful way for their planned gifts. Our goal is to share how much we appreciate you and to acknowledge your generosity in a way that is both comfortable and meaningful to you. Please take the time to answer these questions:

- How would you like to be kept aware of progress being made thanks to your gift or commitment to make a legacy gift?
  - In the annual report? ___yes___no
  - At a party held for donors? ___yes___no

- With a piece of jewelry such as our chapel pin?
  ___yes___no
- While you are at the retreat center? ___yes___no
- Would you like to remain anonymous?
  ___yes___no
- Would you be willing to be interviewed by phone? If so, please share your name and preferred phone number.

  Thank you for the gift of your time.

  _____, Board chair
  _____, Executive Director

Stewardship for large groups of planned givers

When my husband and I agreed to be planned givers for the Girl Scouts, there was a "pinning ceremony." Dianne Belk asked me if Frank wanted a pin too. I told her it wasn't necessary, but Dianne, who had never met my husband, knew him better than I did and brought a pin for him as well. When giving us our pins, Dianne held our hands and looked us in the face and warmly thanked us. The pins were gold daisies, which I am quite sure are not gold. The significance of the daisy is that the founder of the Girl Scouts, Juliette Magill Kinzie Gordon, was affectionately known as "Daisy."

Three weeks later, I was headed to a fundraising training retreat for the Girl Scouts of Western New York. Frank was running around the house tearing it apart, obviously looking for something. When I asked him what he was looking for, he said, "I can't find my daisy pin." Finally the pin was found. Frank and I both showed up with our bling that proudly stated, "We believe in the power of girls to achieve, and we believe the Girl Scouts will get it done. And we have gone the extra mile to make sure it happens."

Stewardship calls

It is far more effective to say thank you over the phone than to write a note. You can have a two-way conversation. There are four parts to a stewardship phone call:
- Share who you are and the reason for the call.
  - Example: "This is Linda Hall. I am a board member for The Humane Society of Rochester and would like to speak to Sarah to thank her for her gift." If the person who has answered the phone is Sarah, continue with: "We really appreciate your gift. This is your tenth year of giving, so happy anniversary as well." Remember, do not say "generous gift" unless you know it was generous. Sarah could have given $1,000 in the morning and bought a $7,000 dress in the afternoon, or she could have saved for ten months to make the gift.
- Ask, "If you have a minute, would you mind sharing why we are so fortunate as to receive your gift?" Then stop talking and listen. Sarah might be a dog person or a cat person. She might be a retired veterinarian or a new pet owner. If she is a new pet owner, ask if she is aware of your services. If a retired veterinarian, ask questions about her practice.

- Ask, "What are we doing well and what can we do better?"
- Make a record of the conversation and have it logged in the donor database. Include any follow-up that is necessary or that you have already done, such as sending a link to your website or setting up coffee because the donor sounds like a great potential board or committee member.

Here is a rough sample of a caller form. See chart on page 190. You might want to add additional data that you would like to have. Also, some people do not want to know the amount, and some organizations do not wish to share it. One neurosurgeon I know answers the statement "I wish it were more" with "I wish it were more too, but I have no idea how much you gave."

Stewardship events

I once went to a stewardship event where my husband and I were the oldest people there by at least 20 years. People were friendly, but there was no program. We weren't even sure why we were there. We knew we had given a capital gift and kept waiting for something to happen. We asked the executive director if there was a program, and she said no. We hit the veggie tray and went home.

Compare that stewardship event to one I heard about from friends at a dinner party. These friends had all made capital gifts to a program that provided pianos

186 · PLANNED GIVING BASICS

Caller:		Date:			
AMOUNT OF GIFT	YEARS OF GIVING	PHONE NUMBER	EMAIL	COMMENTS:
$1,200	5	618-374-5555	amy@gmail.com	Was unavailable. Left message.
$25	1	212-738-4432	MaryAnn32@aol.com	Adopted dog named Scruffy for grandson. Had never been to the Humane Society before. Was impressed by cleanliness. Told her we would send the paper newsletter, per her request.
$500	3	212-714-3529	none	Dog Pookie, age 14, was euthanized. Could not speak highly enough about how kind our staff was, especially Dr. Stan Feldman. Will eventually come back to adopt another pet.
$2,500	22	213-871-3042	Chris@gotbucks.com	Mentioned giving from her family foundation. Set up appointment for August 12 to bring entire family on a tour.

for underprivileged kids. They'd gone to the event more than six months earlier and they were still talking about specific kids, the music they played, and what the kids said the gift of a piano and lessons had done for their attitude toward discipline and their sense of self. Another event was in the works, and rumor had it an incredible prodigy would be playing there. Those of us who hadn't been to the first event asked how we could get invitations to the second one. If I ran the show, it would be time for a planned gift ask. We gave a gift and went to the next stewardship event. The program was at a pre-HDTV venue in a rough part of town. The cuisine consisted of cheese cubes, soda, fruit juice, and no booze, yet we had more fun there than we had at a recently attended gala at a Ritz Carlton. After watching the commitment and joy of both the gifted and not-so-gifted kids who played their hearts out, we left inspired to make another gift.

You need to have a stewardship budget. Staff should not have to pay for a meal out of pocket, but board members should if they are able. Small gifts such as a plaque, book, meal, or plant should be covered in the budget. You might want to have a cap on the money spent on a stewardship gift or meal. I remember one development director who called me ranting about the executive director spending $3,000 on a dinner for four. ($3,000 is not a typo.) After the dinner, the couple didn't make a planned gift. Their original gift was $1,000. Somehow the ED thought that the way to close a gift with wine connoisseurs was with an over-the-top meal. The director of development felt that this kind of profligate spending sent the wrong message. Remember, clever, simple, and meaningful beat expensive and trite. When it comes to working with donors, frequently cheese cubes and an inspiring program trump a five-star meal with wine pairings.

Donor stewardship events are important. Imagine if you made an irrevocable gift to a nonprofit and never heard from them again. You were not informed of the impact of your gift, of future needs, or of new leadership. How likely would you be to:

- Increase your gift?
- Give more during your lifetime?
- Ask others to give?
- Share how wonderful the organization is with your family and friends so that donations at your death would go to this organization?

It is surprising and wonderful how little it takes to make people happy. I was having coffee with a friend. He was given a $15 paperweight from an organization where he had donated his time and money for 20 years. He brought this hunk of metal, which surely did his suit jacket no good, to show me. It had his name on it and "Thanks for Caring." He told me, "I am good for another 20 years."

Anonymous giving

Many people choose to give anonymously. One reason might be fear that they will be bombarded by requests. There are other reasons. A former neighbor, for example, told me that he gave to Planned Parenthood anonymously because his CEO and most of the family-owned company he worked for were pro-life.

When possible, however, you might want to ask donors to reconsider their wish for anonymity. One of my colleagues told a friend who had started her own hedge fund, "We all looked up to you in college. You've done well. In fact, you've done damn well. You set an example for us then. Consider doing it now."

Her former college roommate then agreed to go public. The donor's original thinking was that she didn't want to make classmates who hadn't made a ton of money feel bad. She had great respect for her dorm mates who had decided to go into lower paying but important jobs, such as teaching, nursing, and social work.

Summary

When a planned gift commitment is signed, it is not an end to the relationship between donor and nonprofit. Keep donors up to date, check in on them, and show them the love and respect they have earned from your organization. And remember, simple and experiential gifts trump those that are expensive and trite.

HOW'S THIS FOR A MARKETING SLOGAN?...
"WE'LL TAKE FROM YOU
WHAT YOU CAN'T TAKE WITH YOU"

How to market your planned giving program

We used to live in a simpler world. You could grow your own food, go to a grocery store, or dine at a restaurant. Now, Amazon can deliver it, the restaurants will send it over, you can email your order to the grocery store, you can have the meals delivered with a specific calorie count, gluten or no gluten, and the options go on. The same is true of going to the movies. When I was little, you could go to a drive-in, go to a theater, or wait two years and see the film on TV. There are now an insane number of ways to see a movie or a prize fight or even an opera.

All of this is to say that there are numerous ways to market your planned giving program. The trick is to find out how people want to receive information. Some methods take a big investment. Acquisition mailings or asking one-on-one can be time-consuming; other methods like email will be relatively quick and easy. The trick is to find out what works for your potential legacy givers. You could send out 10,000 emails and get one planned giver, or have four face-to-face interviews and close 100% of the gifts. You will need to measure and monitor costs and outcomes.

Phase 1: If you have no planned giving program

You might want to consider what I call "planned giving lite." This means incorporating two sentences in your annual report, board commitment letter, website, or any other communication:

"If you value the work we do and want the symphony to continue to play great music, or a shelter for victims of domestic violence and their children to continue to turn their lives around, or a place for teens to be safe and productive after school, please consider a gift in your estate plan. For more information call 888-333-XXXX or email us at developmentperson@greatnonprofit.org."

I just worked with a 150-year-old Midwestern organization with a stellar record of service that did not mention planned giving on its website. It turned out that the site was done by a millennial who had never thought of a will, much less of a donation at the end of one's life, whenever that occurs. You need to have groups of different ages and stages of life proofreading your materials. It took five minutes to include a mention of planned giving and its importance on the website. I loved it when the millennial techie said, "In grad school I never learned about marketing to the almost dead." To give this young man his due, he was brilliant when it came to crowdfunding and taught me a lot.

If you incorporate only these two sentences, you will have achieved a lot. Unless you want to go out of business in the next 20 years or believe you already have enough funds, the potential of leaving a planned gift should be part of all your marketing materials

Phase 2

You have already received planned gifts over the years with little to no work. You periodically get a call from an estate attorney who informs you that you are going to get X dollars over the next three years. You do the happy dance and go back to work.

You know you have the kind of programming and reputation that inspire people to leave you in their estate plan. And this is without any effort on your part! It is now time to get serious and intentional. It is time to actively go after planned gifts, starting with your board, major donors, staff, and volunteers.

You will need to put policies and procedures into place. You may be ready to hire a part- or full-time planned giving officer.

Phase 3

You have gifts coming in, a legacy program that acknowledges gifts, and policies and procedures that are up-to-date. Every year, however, brings new donors and board members. Many board members are loath to ask their friends for money. Training needs to continue with board, staff, and volunteers on how to make the ask, how to steward specific donors, and how to make planned giving a part of your organization's culture.

Caveat

Planned giving works better for some organizations than for others because of the difference in their missions. I live across the street from the magnificent Forest Park. It was established in 1876, but major building took place for the 1904 World's Fair. (Now sing along, "Meet me in St. Louie, Louie, meet me at the Fair...") The name of the organization that oversees the park is called Forest Park Forever. It has the future in its title.

Now imagine an organization called "Cancer Forever." Not quite the same ring. Many of your organizations that focus on education, social services, religion, and the arts have a much easier time asking for a planned gift than those focused on specific diseases. I certainly hope that there is a big celebration when the cancer organizations can close their doors. And I hope that I attend the celebration in my lifetime. Some of your reasons for existence will fade away as problems are solved. The more urgent the problem, the sooner you need to raise the money. Most organizations, however, will need to exist for generations to come.

Okay, you have your ducks in a row. How do you encourage people to make a planned gift and share the information with you?

- Start with a marketing plan. Here are the questions you must ask as you write your plan:
  - The big question: Who is your audience? Who do you want to reach and how do they get their information? Remember to start with the proverbial "low-hanging fruit." In the case of planned giving, this means people who have already given to you over a period of years. If they are childless, your chances of a gift improve greatly. If they have grandchildren, your chances decrease dramatically.
  - Do we have a budget item this year for marketing planned giving?
  - If we have funds, how much do we have and what do they cover?
  - If money is nonexistent, will this be a volunteer, staff, or board-driven effort?
  - What are the priorities of our organization for the next year? Will these priorities coordinate or interfere with the launch of planned giving?

  Example: After a capital campaign, is it a good time to go back and ask for a planned gift from the people who have already made a philanthropic investment? Should you go back to the folks who love you but didn't have the cash today?

- How much time, if any, will this take senior management?
- Will senior management not only greenlight the project with money, but will they invest their time?
- Will you make or have you already made a planned gift? Don't even think of asking if you are not giving yourself. Remember the phrase that pays: "Will you join me?"
- Will senior management join you in making a gift?
- What is going on in your field? Federal or state cuts? Opportunities—federal, state, other funders?
- Can you use current marketing staff, or should you hire an outside firm?
- If you have no staff and no funds, can you get pro bono marketing counsel? Remember, free is sometimes too expensive! It can cost you time and effort and you can lose supporters if you don't like their work. On the other hand, you could find the next marketing genius of the century.

- How are you currently marketing your organization?
  - Facebook
  - LinkedIn
  - Twitter
  - Webinars
  - Newsletters, print or online
  - Newspaper ads
  - News releases
  - Brochures

- Billboards
- Lectures
- Tours
- Mission trips
- One-on-one meetings with current loyal donors

The big question: How are you going to track what is working? You might have to do some experimenting. I remember one consulting firm saying, "You have to do this exactly as we say. It is like following your grandmother's recipe. Unless you do it exactly like she did, you won't get the same results." All I could think of was baking my mother's German chocolate cake in Denver, which is a mile high, and producing a pastry that was so hard, it was weapon-grade. The truth is, what works in Manhattan for an opera company might not work in rural Georgia for a food bank. Be prepared to experiment and learn.

Marketing and death

Keep in mind, says colleague Dr. Russell James, that you will get a better response if you tell stories of living people who made charitable bequests rather than tell stories of those who have died.

Example: Liz was the great-granddaughter of a slave and worked as a cleaning woman her entire working life. Her husband was unlucky enough to have been the right age for both World War II and Korea. When he wasn't in the service, he was a union ironworker. Liz and her husband had one son who died at age 52.

Liz worked for one family for more than 20 years. When Liz's husband became ill, the family she worked for helped get him into a nursing home. When he passed away, she was lonely. The family suspected that the daily visits to the nursing home and the relationship with the staff had kept her going. The family asked Liz if she would like a dog. Now retired, Liz thought it was a great idea. After three trips to an animal shelter, she decided on a yappy three-pound puppy she named Princess.

About this time, Liz's former employer asked her what she was going to do with her estate. Startled, Liz informed her that she did not exactly live in Downton Abbey. The woman reminded Liz that she owned a

THERE ARE BETTER WAYS OF ASKING FOR A PLANNED GIFT.

house, a car, savings, and life insurance, and said she'd asked an attorney friend to write a simple will for Liz. When the lawyer asked Liz what she really cared about, she said, "My dog, Princess." When Liz passes away, she will be donating around $175,000, depending on the value of her home and savings, to the shelter where she found her beloved dog. Liz had never given them a dime. Liz planned to leave Princess to her former employer, who was appalled to hear that, since the dog had already bitten through her favorite pair of silk slacks, drawing blood. The family agreed that when the time came they would find Princess a good home and, in the meantime, suggested some doggie training.

Hints for specific marketing techniques

- *Billboards:* Nearly everyone who drives the highways of Missouri knows about Ann's Bra Stores. Why? Because of its billboards. When customers come into the store, a saleswoman will ask how they heard about it. Sometimes the answer is a referral from a doctor for mastectomy patients. But the key driver of new business are those billboards. Don't shrink from going "old school."
- *Direct mail:* When do your donors feel flush? The time varies wildly from place to place. Hedge fund managers know in January—when they receive their bonuses—how much money they made the previous year. Farmers are paid when the crops come in. Many older donors respond better to direct mail. Remem-

ber, mature donors are your target for planned giving, not millennials.

- *At Events:* Can you tie the launch of your planned giving campaign with another event, or is it better to spearhead the campaign on its own? Planned giving and golf are usually not a good combo, especially if the weather is hot and the booze is plentiful. If the golfers are invited by vendors or clients, they might not even know what organization the tournament sponsors. Also, women make 82% of all philanthropic decisions, but they make up only 22% of golfers. If they are not on the golf course, it's not a good time.
- *Annual gala:* This might be a great time to announce your campaign, present a short speech, and tell guests there is more information to come. Be sure to have information in your program book about whom to contact. Use language that aligns with your beliefs. If you believe, for example, that everyone should have the chance to live without fear of violence, consider a planned gift to our organization. Call our development director, Maria Jose Kessler, at 636-292-3056 or email her at patti@greatdevelopmentofficer.edu.
- *Informational event*: Here you attract a content-driven rather than party-driven crowd. This event, hosted by a board member and presided over by the CEO, might give an update on major medical breakthroughs in a certain disease or information from

experts in your field. I remember a lecture given in 1984 by Adam Pinsker, then-executive director of Dance St. Louis. The talk was so fascinating I remember it to this day. (And I can't remember what I had for breakfast this morning!) I would have seriously considered a planned gift if I had been asked.

- *Print advertising:* People who read obituaries tend to read them daily. The readers are in your ideal age group and potential planned givers. Consider an ad to run in the obituary section like this: "According to Dr. Russell James, people who make charitable gifts in their wills live longer. Consider a planned gift to OurWonderfulOrganization.org. To find out more call Holly Hall at 202-345-6281." Another example: "What do you want your legacy to be? If you care about the future of education, check out GreatEducation.org. or call Lily Seymore at 382-912-2222.

Try different approaches and see if the phone rings.

Touring for dollars

Train your tour guides. It doesn't matter if your donors are visiting you around the corner or halfway around the world. You can't sell what you don't know. Clinique doesn't do it. Apple doesn't do it. Boeing doesn't do it. Why should your nonprofit do it? Tour training should include dispelling common misconceptions about your organization.

During tour training for a senior facility, I asked the intake workers two questions: What are the most common misconceptions about your home? How can you reeducate your visitors during the tour?

This facility had been a home for retired nuns, and in the entryway hung photos of the sisters who had once lived there. I suggested they replace the photos of the nuns with those of the married couples and the single men and women who were living there now. I also suggested that the intake workers start the tour with a statement such as, "The most common misconception about our home is that we only serve one order. Twenty years ago, we expanded to 12 orders. Then ten years ago, we opened our doors to women, and five years ago we welcomed men and married couples. Today, 5% of our residents are men and 18% are not even Catholic."

Ideally, your potential donor should experience the mission firsthand. What impression do you want to convey to your potential planned givers when they tour your facilities or visit a country where you are working? Some facilities are real dumps, which makes it clear that help is needed. I once worked with a senior living center that looked like pre-war Tara from *Gone with the Wind*. No one would guess that stipends were needed for residents who run out of funds. One of the residents shared with me that her son, an orthopedic surgeon, had been paying for her stay. At age 39, he died of a cerebral aneurysm, and he died without a will. His wife was not a fan of her mother-in-law and refused to continue paying her fees. Thanks to the endowment, the woman could continue to stay at her senior center.

Are all visitors given the same spiel? Is a potential donor treated the same as a potential client? Does any thought go into planning the outcome of the tour? What do you want your visitor to do when they leave your agency? Tim Gunn, host of *Project Runway*, has written marvelous fashion books that talk about his time at The Fashion Institute of Technology in Manhattan. When visitors commented on what a mess the place was and how it needed painting, Tim was offended. If you know Tim, or meet him, please let him know that this was the perfect time to say, "I couldn't agree with you more. We choose to keep tuition low rather than spend it on repainting the place. Would you be interested in talking to someone from our development staff about getting it painted? Nothing would make us happier."

Before a mission trip, make sure that your potential donors know what to expect. Having unrealistic expectations of food and lodging or the amount of walking involved can result in illness or injury, putting a kibosh on your future relations. A letter such as this eases the way:

Dear Cris and John,

I cannot wait to show you the Children's Eternal Rainforest. Costa Rica is breathtaking in the fall. You will be amazed at what your last seven years of support—the trees you have purchased—have done to stop erosion. You will be both thrilled at the progress of reforestation and surprised at how far we still must go to save the lungs of the earth.

As we discussed, your knowledge of hydrogeology and ornithology will be invaluable to the group. I am so glad you like rice and beans. The food is wonderful—simple and freshly made. There is a list of clothing and specialized items you will want to bring. The most important thing to remember is that it is the rainy season, so you will need wet weather clothing and DEET to ward off mosquitos. Our travel agent, Anne Volland, will send you a note regarding the details. If you have any questions, and can't get the answers you need from Anne, please don't hesitate to call me on my cell, 314-863-4422. We are going to have an amazing time!

Sincerely,
Laurie Waller
President, Friends of the Children's Eternal Rainforest

After prepping your tour members, prep the tour guides. When working with The Children's Eternal Rainforest in Costa Rica, I asked the guide what he usually does the first night. He said he tells visitors what they are going to see on the tour. I asked him if he wanted to help me raise the maximum amount of money possible, as well as make his largest tips.

That got his attention. I suggested that he ask the visitors what *they* wanted to see and what would be a high point for them on the tour. He followed my suggestion. Emilio, our little brother from Big Brothers, Big Sisters who came with us, said that he wanted to see every poisonous snake in Costa Rica. My goal was to see no poisonous snakes. Some people were interested in flora, some fauna. One woman said that holding a sloth would make this a perfect trip. Our guide listened closely. He made sure Emilio saw snakes and Kate held a sloth. And sure enough, the guide told me that he had never received such generous tips. Plus, we had the commitment of the group for further major donor support. Next stop: planned giving.

For those of you who have a nondescript office, rather than a rainforest to share with your potential donors, photographs of your work can tell the story. First ask your visitor what he or she knows about your organization. This is the first opportunity to correct misinformation. Even if nothing comes up, the next step is to dispel any misconceptions.

In 1991, neonatal nurse Sharon Rohrbach founded Nurses for Newborns, because she wanted follow-up for high-risk infants. Sharon was a charismatic leader who eventually attracted the attention of two well-known and powerful women: Oprah Winfrey and Laura Bush. They both endorsed her work; Oprah donated $100,000. That is a lot of money, but it was a one-time gift. Great press followed, and, as a result, the referrals went up and the giving went down. The assumption of many donors appeared to be that if you have Oprah as a donor, why do you need little old me? We had photos of Sharon and the two powerful women on the wall. She began the tour explaining the results of their attention: More clients, less money.

You also must pay close attention to the photos on which your visitors focus. The wife of a prominent CEO new to the area came to visit Nurses for Newborns, and was deeply touched by a photo of an infant living in a shopping cart. She asked about the family. The staff said that the mother was homeless, and the grocery cart was in lieu of a crib. That photo was worth more than a thousand words. To date, it has been worth more than one million dollars—the amount this visitor and her husband donated. Little did the staff know at the time that the CEO's wife had once been a nurse and that she understood what it meant to live in poverty.

Lessons learned:

- Don't rush through your tour. Remember that you don't have to share every aspect of your operation and history on the first visit. Concentrate on what the donor wants to know, not on what you feel a need to share. On a first visit, your potential donor might not care about your organization's founder or tax status but would rather hear about current programs and future plans.

- Pay attention to the expressions of your visitors, whether quizzical, sad, or bored.
- Ask questions. With the woman staring at the photo of the baby in the shopping cart, a simple "What are you thinking?" yielded deep and transformative information.
- Ask in advance if there is a specific topic the visitor wants to explore or a particular staff person the visitor would like to get to know. Some people want to talk to clinical staff; others, to the CFO or development director.
- Don't make assumptions. Always ask, "What do you know about our organization and mission?" There is no need to explain to a physician the definition of breast cancer or tuberculosis, or to the Ph.D. director of a botanical garden the method of plant procreation. (I have seen tour guides make both blunders.)
- Every organization needs a wish list. It can include just about anything, from diapers and secretarial services to tracts of land and multimillion-dollar buildings. The list should be updated and circulated to everyone in the organization, including clients and volunteers, and it should be posted in your facilities. Everyone involved in the organization should have an opportunity to contribute to the list. Many years ago, I was president of a board whose wish list included paving for our parking lot. A new board member who was in the construction busi-

ness saw the wish list in the men's restroom. He had the parking lot paved, pro bono, within the week.

For those of you who have been to London and ridden the tube (what Brits call their subway), the recording announces, "Mind the Gap." I have the same message: Mind the Gap. Where is the gap, or, in other words, where is the continuing need and how can you bring it to the forefront of the people who are touring? What is your vision? Do you have a wish list?

It might sound something like this: "At XYZ agency, thanks to the generosity of our donors, we are proud to serve 900 hot meals a day. Our goal is to serve 2,000 a day. Many people in our parish are still going hungry."

The trick at this point is to stop walking and talking and wait for questions. If there are none, move on. However, you just might hear, "What do you need?" This is your opportunity to fill the gap with your wish list and give your visitor a way to get involved. I had a client in Texas who used this technique with a rancher who was touring a residential care facility for victims of domestic violence. When the rancher heard what the facility needed, he sent a freezer and an entire cow with a note that said, "Let me know when it's all eaten, and I'll send you another one." (Apologies to my vegan and vegetarian readers, but I think this was a triumph.)

Always leave lots of time for questions. When I worked with the New Mexico Wildlife Center, Melissa Moore, the ED, took me on a private tour of the facility.

In the medical wing, she was about to tell me how many animals would fit into their Isolate. I am not a medical professional, but I am a mother and grandmother and noticed that the incubator was patched with duct tape. My husband and sons swear by duct tape as an international cure-all, but frankly it scares me.

So I asked Melissa, "What's with the duct tape?" She said that she was so used to seeing it, she had forgotten it was there. She then explained that the Wildlife Center needed at least three to four Isolates, but they were very expensive. I asked if gently-used incubators would work—in other words, ones without duct tape. When she said "yes," we spent the next 15 minutes talking about how to get used incubators. I took a pledge to make sure they had Isolates for the baby animals in need of them. Was this part of Melissa's planned tour? No. Does she want injured baby animals to have better outcomes? Yes. What she did that was so perfect: She stopped talking and let me share my concerns. (I haven't located any affordable incubators, meaning free or available for paying the shipping costs. If you know of any, please call me at 314-863-4422 or email me at carol@boardbuilders.com.)

Just as you give your visitors an opportunity to discover how they can financially fill the gap, you must be able to describe your vision to your clients or patrons. For instance, standing in an empty theater, your tour guide might say, "We would like every audience member to have the opportunity to experience the premiere of an emerging playwright. Just imagine being in the audience when Tennessee Williams, David Mamet, or Sam Shepard debuted a work that changed the face of theater. All in this lovely little space."

Then stop talking and listen. Find out what your potential donor cares about. Is experimental theater even of interest? Is this a *My Fair Lady* kind of person? You might not be a fit at all or, you can ask, what do you like about *My Fair Lady*? If your potential donor says that she used to be a dancer and loves musicals with a lot of dancing, ask her if she would like to be contacted if one is being considered for debut. This might be the kind of program your donor would want to finance and eventually endow through a planned gift. And sometimes, it just isn't a fit and you have to say to your donor, "Thank you for your time." Ask if s(he) has any friends who might interested," and say to yourself, "Next!"

Written materials

Whether writing a brochure, newsletter, or website copy, stress how your donors don't have to be on the Forbes 100 list to make their dreams come true. Acknowledge that donors can take care of themselves and their families and still have enough to aid a cause they cherish. Share the stories of current donors who are alive and shaping visions. And have contact information for someone in your organization or affiliated with you who can help donors find the best way to make their planned gifts.

Summary

Your potential donor will make the ultimate decision from the heart, not the head. It is your job to find out how they receive information and to use those channels. There are certainly tax advantages to giving to a favorite charity rather than to the government, but, ultimately, donors must feel the love and own the dream. Whether it is a community with access to education for all, a lab dedicated to ending dental disease, a city where children with mental health problems can get care, or a world where music is heard and celebrated, you can make the dream happen when you ask.

SOMETIMES, ALPHABET SOUP
DOESN'T GO DOWN WELL.

10

What are you going to ask for

I couldn't have written this chapter without the counsel of Dianne Johnson, JD. The stories and information herein are meant to illustrate broad generalities; the laws and regulations vary state to state and are constantly changing. When you find yourself blessed enough to help your donors, please remain open and ask for help yourself. Also, this book is written to reflect the U.S. law as we know it the day we go to press. Laws change, tax codes change, and this section is not applicable to the laws of other countries.

Percentage or amount to give

First let's talk about an issue that often arises when talking with a donor. Donors more and more want to designate gifts for a specific purpose, and they may also want to give a specific amount. If the donor is young and the goal specific, the amount may or may not cover his or her intent. For instance, if the donor wants to leave $100,000 to build a playground for a pre-school with the goal of safe activities for small children, and the donor dies in 40 years, the cost might be $2 million, which is much more than the gift. Also, the school could already have a playground by then or have been razed altogether.

If the donor is 85, the chances of this happening are less, but if you have ever built or rehabbed a house or watched HGTV, you know that prices can go up faster than a speeding bullet. So, if you can achieve a less restricted gift, such as "purchase equipment to ensure a high level of activity for children," your donor's wishes have a better chance of being met and everyone will be happier. Also: Recommending to the donor that making their charitable gift a percentage of their estate or a percentage of an asset will ensure the value of the gift keeps up with the changing costs, from the time the gift is written to the time it is realized.

Another issue is to avoid giving a naming right in perpetuity. One of my colleagues who works for an international botanical garden often gets asked to name a tree in honor of a donor or a donor's family member. When confirming the gift, the garden staff always makes sure the donor understands that the memorial tree or planting is guaranteed for only 20 years. Trees and bushes do not live forever and buildings will eventually be torn down, so it is important that donors know that no gift or naming is forever.

Also, wiring, safety regulations, and other mandated changes can be expensive. There is a hospital right now in a large city where a 30+ story tower is not earthquake-proof. It met the requirements when built, but not now. There is no provision in the agreement between the institution and the donor regarding how long the donor's name remains on the building. As a result, the heirs are entangled in an ongoing legal battle regarding the name that will grace the new tower.

Some folks ask for a percentage of a donor's estate. You might consider a "1% Club," which is composed of people who have left a gift of 1% or more to your organization. Ninety-nine percent of us are not in the 1% of the wealthiest people in our country, so this is a somewhat whimsical way to enter a 1% group. Your donors are more likely to feel that there is enough money both to live on and to give to their inheritors if your charity is getting "only" 1%.

Frankly, if my husband and I die in a plane crash, there will be lots of money for our heirs and charities. If we have prolonged illnesses that require round-the-clock nursing care, our kids and charities will be in a much different position. The bottom line is that no one knows, which is why we are comfortable giving a percentage. If or when we get into our 80s or 90s, we might make major changes. This is why wills and trusts are written on paper and not etched in stone.

How donors want to give gifts

There is nothing wrong with receiving a check when your organization is named in a will or trust, but your donor might have had other assets that would reduce the amount of income or estate tax that their inheritors or estate will have to pay. Specific assets that a donor might transfer, other than an outright cash designation, include:

- Life insurance policies
- Retirement accounts
- Appreciated stock
- Real estate
- Collectibles
- Art
- Shares in privately owned businesses

It is important to have a bare-bones knowledge of how assets are disbursed at the time of death. Unless you ensure your donor receives expert advice and you have some idea of the potential for the estate to fulfill the donor's desires, both your charity and your donor's family might get far less than expected. About 90% of all gifts are simple bequests and transfer through a will or trust. If the asset, like a bank account, stock brokerage account, or real estate, is held only in the donor's name, then it will pass on through a will or probate. This is the first way that assets and cash can pass to inheritors. There may be tax advantages to your donors to consider, however, which impact what assets to give and alternate ways of giving. More on those later.

First let's review the other ways that donors' assets can pass on to inheritors: See chart on page 226.

(Note: These are broad generalities, and you should always consult a financial professional for your individual situation.)

The second way that we bequeath assets is commonly referred to as "transfer on death or payable on death." This method includes joint tenancy, which is a fancy way of saying "ownership." Hence the old saying, "Possession is nine tenths of the law." When we pass away, any assets that we own *with* someone else's name listed on the title automatically become theirs. By definition, when we are no longer here, the asset becomes theirs as the remaining joint owner.

Many find that making a gift of assets via "changing the title" is significantly easier than making a charitable bequest through a will or trust. When your donor titles his or her assets, there is a significant upside including:

- There are no lawyer fees to move assets.
- There is no statutory waiting period.
- The family can begin the healing process without being hassled by bill collectors.
- You, the nonprofit, have the assurance that your donor's wish to include you is fulfilled in a timely manner with little to no cost to you or the family.

Let's look at some of the more common ways that titling works.

The first is Joint Trust with Rights of Survivorship (JTWROS); the other is Transference on Death (TOD) or Payable on Death (POD). JTWROS essentially means when one person passes, the ownership shifts proportionately to the other owners. If there were three people who initially owned something together, they each owned one third. When one of them dies and there are only two owners, those two each own one half.

TOD & POD are often used interchangeably. When talking with your donor about leaving money to your organization, however, remember that TODs tend to be tangible assets. So, if your donor has a boat, s(he) might want to TOD the boat to your organization for you to use or sell as you see fit. PODs are assets that are converted to cash and then given to your organization. For our purposes, we will use them interchangeably. When you are talking with your donor, however, you will want to remember the differences.

The reason to inquire about the assets left to your organization is that you might not want a specific item if the use is restricted. For instance, if the donor wants to donate a boat to your summer program, but you are planning to sell your lakeside summer camp, a boat makes little sense. You can then discuss whether s(he) might allow you to sell the boat and buy something appropriate for your new recreational facility.

You could also politely inquire whether (s)he was titling the asset to your organization or via TOD/POD.

This can open a conversation that allows you to advocate for the needs of your organization, as well as make sure that your donor's wishes are honored.

When valuable items are not properly assigned, there can be family challenges. When my mother died, she left behind some anti-Jewish propaganda books that she was translating for a symposium. They were frightening because the beautiful illustrations were hate-filled and aimed at children. When Mom died, the books had not been assigned. I suggested to my siblings that we give them to the St. Louis Holocaust Museum. They immediately agreed.

The Museum was thrilled with the gift because 1) Our notarized letter stated that they could do anything they wanted with the books, including selling or trading them; 2) The letter was signed by all four of the Weisman heirs; 3) There was a letter of provenance, albeit in German; and 4) We did not care about or ask for a tax benefit. The director was thrilled because they had some of the books in the series but not others, and could trade them with other museums. Had one or more of my siblings not agreed, we could have been headed to court. Invariably, items get left out of estate plans.

(Note: These are broad generalities, and you should always consult with an attorney for your individual situation.)

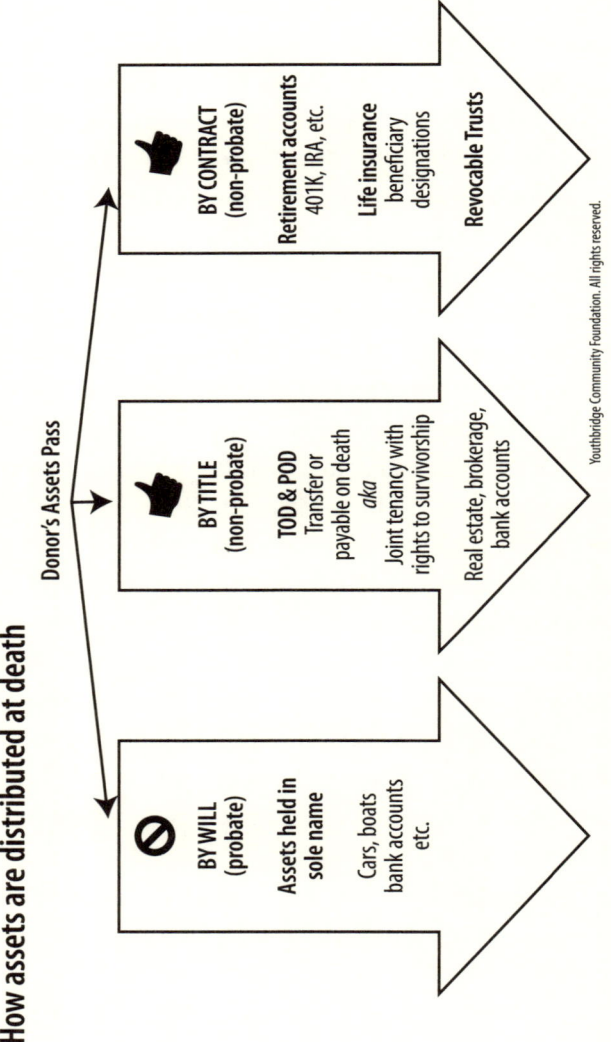

How assets are distributed at death

Donor's Assets Pass

🚫 BY WILL (probate)
Assets held in sole name

Cars, boats, bank accounts etc.

✋ BY TITLE (non-probate)
TOD & POD
Transfer or payable on death
aka
Joint tenancy with rights to survivorship

Real estate, brokerage, bank accounts

✋ BY CONTRACT (non-probate)
Retirement accounts 401K, IRA, etc.

Life insurance beneficiary designations

Revocable Trusts

Youthbridge Community Foundation. All rights reserved.

The third way our personal property transfers is via Contract or Agreement, usually through a Trust or a Beneficiary designation on retirement accounts and life insurance policies. For most donors, Beneficiary designations are likely the simplest and easiest method.

What is a Trust? A Trust is a legal entity that can own your donor's stuff before, during, and after their death. They come in quite handy, as they allow donors to avoid the probate process. Remember probate? It's like going to the DMV every day for four months. Or maybe six months. Then one more day.

A Trust is also a legal arrangement that allows donors to make their wishes known after death. This can include instructions about what they do *not* want to happen to their stuff, as well as who is to receive it and when. The last component can even include conditions under which disbursements from the Trust would have to be returned. An example: They donated land for wildlife research, and four years later the organization decides to open a brothel on the farm instead. While the lifestyle may be wild, this would clearly violate the donor's wishes. This is the penultimate donor intent. What a wonderful way to help donors see that even in death they still have control over how their assets are used. Pretty cool, right?

At the extreme, a Trust allows for "control from the grave." Most often, however, it is used to allow your donor to bypass Probate, stay liquid, pay appropriate creditors and final bills, settle affairs privately, and fulfill charitable wishes—all while reducing exposure to criminals, nosy neighbors, abusive creditors, and probate trolls. A Trust may also help donors accomplish their philanthropic, personal, family, and estate-planning goals. You are positioned to share with donors that they may be making a choice without even realizing it, that by not considering a Trust they are unknowingly risking their assets going to banks, lawyers, and the government rather than to their heirs and trusted charities.

Two types of basic Trusts: Revocable and Irrevocable

Revocable Trusts are just like they sound: Donors can make changes while they are alive. They can change a spouse, add a child, or ditch their brother-in-law. Because we never know what life may bring, or how many spouses we might have over the next 20+ years, most people opt for this type. Upon death, by law, it automatically becomes Irrevocable, meaning the ousted brother-in-law cannot try to make changes and add himself to the Trust. Revocable Trusts are a flexible tool for donors that can be modified throughout their lifetimes as circumstances change. You can also assure donors that if there are "named assets" in their Revocable Trust, and for some reason the donor or the family needs those resources, they can still access them during the donor's life. Many donors think a Revocable Trust means that, after their death, anyone in their family can revoke or change it. Be sure to emphasize to donors and families that gifts become irrevocable *only* once the donor is deceased, and that donors can make changes at any time.

If Revocable Trusts are such great tools, why would donors consider an Irrevocable Trust?

Suspend reality for a moment and pretend your donor is Mark Zuckerberg. Regrettably, someone sues him for promoting "fake news" on Facebook that caused a presidential candidate to lose the election. While this may or may not seem implausible, in the court of law stranger things have happened. So let's say that Mark loses his battle in court and must pay $47 billion to the defeated candidate. Now what? If the assets are in a Revocable Trust, your donor is likely "viewed to be in control of those assets," meaning he must access those monies to make good on the legal judgment. But what if he put those shares of FB into an *Irrevocable Trust* years prior to any knowledge of the allegations? He can assert that he had no way of foreseeing any of the events that took place. This means those valuable shares of stock are safe from any legal action and/or potential creditors. The downside would be that, if Mark changed spouses or charities, his Irrevocable Trust likely would not!

Please humor me while I state the obvious: *This is one of the many times you should recommend that you and your donors seek professional guidance on their available options. Some options may be more appropriate than others.*

Beneficiary designations

Beneficiary designations are a fantastic way for your donor to give monies away. These account types have named beneficiaries, and your charity can be one too. They are easy to create and to change during the donor's lifetime. Usually, all it takes is to fill out one piece of paper that lists the beneficiary's name, birth date, % of account paid out. Then sign, date, and mail.

Examples of vehicles that ask donors to name a beneficiary include:

- 401k, 403b, 457
- Traditional IRA
- Roth IRA
- Simple IRA
- SEP (Simplified Employee Pension Plan)
- SARSEP (Salary Reduction Simplified Employee Pension Plan)
- Life Insurance
- Buy-Sell Agreements
- Thrift Savings Plan

Consider including a simple document with your planned giving material that includes this list or one like it. Imagine a conversation where you refer to beneficiary designations in a general way. Some donors may lack the in-depth knowledge of what can be used as a charitable giving vehicle and the resulting tax implications. When you put a list like this in front of a donor, it helps them think more comprehensively of the myriad ways they could include your nonprofit in their plans. Furthermore, there may be large tax benefits to the donor's heirs by naming your nonprofit on tax deferred retirement accounts versus donating cash in the bank.

Think about this for a moment. For most people, their home is their largest asset. If not their home, then most likely it's their retirement accounts. When the accounts were originally opened, the donors named beneficiaries. But time goes on, and people and situations change. Maybe your donor remarried after being divorced or widowed. Or maybe the donor took a new job and has "money in motion." This is a perfect opportunity to change that beneficiary to a charity.

Let me explain: First, it is a simple process to make someone the beneficiary of an IRA, life insurance policy, etc. It is commonly changed through a "change of beneficiary form," and usually consists of:

- your name
- date of birth
- account number
- name(s) of each beneficiary
- their dates of birth
- percentage of the account you wish to bequest them

It probably takes longer to find a pen than to fill out the form. The donor signs it, dates it and drops it in the mail. It is that simple. No lawyers. No legal fees. No hassles.

226 · PLANNED GIVING BASICS

Second, your donor may believe that everything is being taken care of through their will. But is it? If your donor named his or her "estate" as the beneficiary, the IRA is now immediately taxable in full, which means you wind up in a higher tax bracket and beneficiaries receive less. And your nonprofit? A much smaller gift.

Third, what do most adult children do when they inherit their parent's wealth? For starters, they may be required to pay taxes on retirement accounts, and then they often spend much of the balance. So if your donor has three children, s(he) would normally leave each of them 33 1/3%.

What if you could show your donor a better way? Maybe leave each kid 30%, and leave 10% to your nonprofit? Would each kid really miss the 3 1/3% after taxes? Many donors with adult children recognize that the kids plan on spending their money. Potential donors sometimes hold onto money they do not want, or will never need and never spend, just so they do not have to witness the children spending their money. Emotional blackmail is also a reason some folks hold onto money that is not needed. Junior's visits, for example, may be motivated by a basketful of money. For some, money equates to love and can be used as a weapon.

Fourth, let's consider other employer-sponsored account types that typically list beneficiaries, namely:
- Stock options
- Restricted stock

- Phantom stock
- Group life insurance

These assets are generally not held inside a retirement account, and thus they are almost always fully taxable upon passing *unless* given to charity. This is a compelling option since your goal is to help solve a problem that your donors may not even realize they have. You can show your donors where they could have a large tax bill looming for their heirs. By guiding them through a basic conversation on these types of vehicles, you will win their confidence and secure their loyalty for years to come.

Remember, most people have their home as their greatest asset. Who gets the house? This is where having a Gift Acceptance Policy comes in handy. If a home is the only asset your donor has, and you feel that your organization can accept and dispose of a gift of real estate, then by all means, accept the gift. Some organizations will not accept gifts of real estate because they are too complex and costly to deal with. Unless they liquidate quickly, homes can become a liability for the organization (think utility bills, insurance, real estate taxes, etc.). Often a donor will have retirement assets as well as assets of physical property and/or equipment within an estate. Help your donor see that accepting the retirement assets is likely a better option for both you and the donor, by explaining the following:

- You do not need to wait for a house to sell in order to collect your gift.
- The kids will pay income taxes on the IRAs, 401(k)s, etc., but not if they receive the house instead. Conversely, a 501(c)3 pays no taxes on gifted IRAs.

Trusts versus online wills

Donors often wonder why they should pay for an attorney when they can do a will online for little or no cost. It's a valid question, and one you should be prepared to address.

- Pro: Inexpensive
- Con: Sometimes free costs too much
- Pro: Quick and easy from the convenience of your couch
- Con: Is this really something you want to do while watching Game of Thrones?
- Pro: An online will is better than no will
- Con: Maybe—but does WebMD make you a doctor?

Please pardon me while I point out the obvious. If your donor honestly cannot afford the roughly $1,500 to $2,500 to hire a properly trained professional, then I highly suggest you re-read the section on Titling. Much of what donors want to accomplish can likely be accomplished if assets are titled appropriately. This approach will demonstrate you have their best interests in mind and create the opportunity for stewardship.

Charitable trusts—the alphabet soup of planned giving

Someone once asked me: In one sentence, why should I consider a planned giving program?

My answer: Planned Giving allows you to ask for *assets* instead of *money*.

Think of it like this: Which is more valuable?
- Your car?
- Your home?
- Your retirement accounts?
- Your life insurance proceeds?
- Your private family business?

Is the cash in your pocket or checking account worth more than your home or retirement accounts?

As mentioned, cash is often one's smallest asset. If you want to raise more money, ask for assets, not cash.

There are two main reasons donors tend to give from the cash bucket:
- That is what they were asked for.
- Few donors want to give away something they are still using.

Simply put, ask if your organization can have an asset when the donor is finished using it.

While explaining a planned gift, put yourself in your donor's shoes and answer this question: "Why would I do this"?

The answer: A monthly income stream *or* a tax deduction *or* maybe both!

Imagine the possibilities when your donor can make a gift to your nonprofit today, receive a tax deduction, and still earn a monthly income on the money they gave away. What if your donor neither needs nor wants the income? Even better! Your organization can earn the income. When done thoughtfully, your donors can give to their favorite nonprofits, and their heirs may inherit as if the donor hadn't given at all!

Donors can give you a dollar and potentially still pass $1 onto their heirs, when previously their heirs would have received only what was left of the dollar *after* taxes. That's right. When done correctly, parents can give money to your charity and leave even more money to their kids. Again, you will need to involve in this discussion a professional advisor who is current on estate and tax laws.

And don't forget, this is not a "one and done." Tax laws change, and what might work well today might not be the best for you, your family, or your donors. You might also recommend that donors check in ever three or four years.

While there are many ways to say it, let's start with what Dr. Russell James calls, "Trade a gift for income." Dr. James has a fantastic way to break this into small bites, so grab your spoon and let's take a deeper look at the various instruments that makes up the Alphabet Soup of Planned Giving.

First, let's choose where the income should come from. Does your donor require an income back from the gift? If no, then please accept the gift and say thank you. If yes, where do they want that income to come from? There are three basic options:
- Income generated from only their gifted assets (CRT)
- Income generated from a pool of various donors (PIF)
- Income guaranteed by your charity (CGA)

Income is hard to grasp but taxes are relatively straightforward

Lowering taxes is great for your donor and great for your organization. When asking for gifts from the "big buckets" (instead of cash), you can create an opportunity for your donor to give more by giving pre-tax assets. This way the donor will receive a larger deduction and you receive a larger gift.

When asking donors if they would like to reduce their taxes, you must be clear about which taxes they want to reduce:
- Capital gains taxes
- Income taxes
- Estate taxes

By asking if your donor has any investments with large gains, they can donate those highly appreciated assets directly to you, thereby never *personally* selling them, so *they* never pay capital gains taxes on these monies. The benefit: You just solved your donor's capital gains tax problem because your charity receives the entire proceeds from the sale (minus transaction costs), making it more affordable for your donor. Donors simply need to decide if their circumstances require an income from that gift, or if they would rather enhance the impact of their generosity and let your organization earn the income.

Desiree is an astute investor who owns a highly appreciated investment, wants to sell it, and wishes to make a cash gift with the proceeds. Two years ago, she purchased 1,000 shares of ABC stock at $20/share, and now it is worth $100/share. Let's look at the capital gains tax math:

Proceeds from sale	$100,000
Minus 'cost basis'	- 20,000
Capital gains	$80,000
Minus 20% Capital gain tax	- 16,000
Proceeds left to donate	$84,000

Donor Benefit

Tax deduction on gift (39.6% bracket)	$33,264
Minus capital gains taxes paid	- 16,000
Total tax reduction to Donor	**$17,264**
Total Benefit to Your Nonprofit	**$84,000**

Now, let's take a look at using assets as the gift instead of the cash proceeds:

Value of stock donation.............................$100,000
Taxes paid by your nonprofit.................- 0
Total Benefit to Your Nonprofit..................**$100,000**

Donor benefit of tax deduction on his or her gift (39.6% bracket)

$100,000
x 39.6%
$39,600

As the math demonstrates, both parties are significantly better off using tax-heavy assets rather than after-tax cash. Now, what if Desiree wanted to give cash instead and not sell her stocks? She simply uses

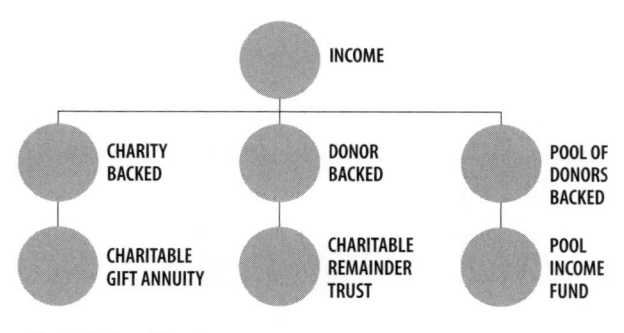

```
                        INCOME
           ┌───────────────┼───────────────┐
        CHARITY          DONOR         POOL OF
        BACKED           BACKED        DONORS
                                       BACKED
           │               │               │
       CHARITABLE      CHARITABLE        POOL
       GIFT ANNUITY    REMAINDER       INCOME
                       TRUST            FUND
```

(Chart 1, Dr. Russell James)

the cash on hand to re-purchase her former shares. Since she never actually sold them, the 30-day wash sale rule does not apply. She would also pick up the added benefit of a higher cost basis on her new ABC shares, thus resulting in a lower capital gain tax should she decide to sell them later.

There are multiple ways to reduce income taxes, the most common being a charitable deduction on a 1040 tax return. Let's look at the other ways that donors can make a commitment for a gift to be given later yet receive an income tax deduction today. These include the charitable remainder trust, charitable lead trust,

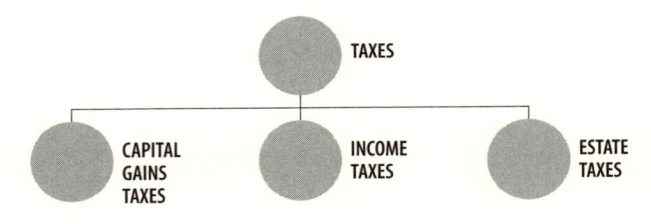

```
                    TAXES
          ┌───────────┼───────────┐
      CAPITAL      INCOME      ESTATE
      GAINS        TAXES       TAXES
      TAXES
```

(Chart 2, Dr. Russell James)

and remainder interest deed from real estate. Remember, donors can still lower their taxes and receive an income from their gifts.

Not only can you help lower income taxes for your donors, you can also lower taxes for their heirs by helping your donors understand that different sources of gifts have different tax implications for their kids. Tax-heavy assets are spectacular gifts for your charity—think retirement accounts.

Let's use the proverbial millionaires next door, Cindy & Abdul. Their home is worth $400,000. They have $100,000 in the bank, and $500,000 in an old 401k. They decide to leave their daughter the retirement account, and their son gets the house and CDs. Who would receive more money?

The son. Why? Because retirement accounts have never been taxed, and the IRS wants to collect taxes when those assets move, making them tax-heavy by IRS design. Now the daughter must pay income taxes on the inherited retirement account, but the son pays no income taxes on an inherited house or cash. And neither would your charity for inheriting the IRAs, which is why you want to ask for tax-heavy assets as gifts.

You can also help your donors lower their estate taxes since money, houses, farms, coins, art, etc., left to your charity at death, passes outside the estate and thus is not taxable. You can even help structure a CRT with an Irrevocable Life Insurance Trust (ILIT) and remove the tax on life insurance left to heirs or to your nonprofit organization (NPO). And don't forget a nongrantor Charitable Lead Trust allows donors to pass on to their heirs without taxation any growth above the IRS-approved stated interest rate.

By themselves, all these planned giving vehicles are easy and straightforward. Ironically, this area is also the toughest part of planned giving since 1) It deals with tax law; 2) Tax laws change frequently; and 3) It takes highly trained professionals to put all this together, so please don't try this at home.

Yet this is likely the place you can be of most financial value to your donors; If they are not working with a professional, refer one to them. Please be prepared to lead the conversation with thoughtful, generative questions to your donor and to their CPA, estate-planning attorney, or wealth manager. Showing them the diagrams in this chapter may prove helpful. I cannot stress this enough: When you get to these types of advanced planned gifts, it behooves you to realize this is above your pay grade and bring in a qualified professional!

Now let's explore what happens when we start stacking these gifts on top of each other. While it sounds more complicated, it isn't. We are still doing the same two things financially: lowering taxes and trading a gift for an income stream.

Desiree could transfer highly appreciated stock into a Charitable Remainder Uni-Trust (CRUT), paying out 9% of the gifts assets back to your donor, at which point the donor can use that income to pay life insurance proceeds on a policy held within an Irrevocable Life Insurance Trust (ILIT). The Charitable Remainder Trust (CRT) eventually transfers all the remaining assets to your charity, while the Life Insurance pays the children (or your NPO) the Life Insurance proceeds. Etc, etc, etc. It is still the same two things. Easy peasy, lemon squeezy.

(Note: Since our research shows that less than 10% of planned gifts utilize the higher-end tactics of CGA, CRAT, CRUT, Uni-Trust, etc., our discussion focused on the most popular of these giving vehicles and thus is not an all-inclusive review. For a more thorough explanation of all giving vehicles of this type, read Dr. Russell James' book, "Visual Planned Giving.")

Colleague and friend Michael McMurtrey shares this story:

"Roughly three decades ago, my father used a unique approach to help someone. He donated highly appreciated company stock to an Educational Uni-Trust. For three years, the Uni-Trust paid 9% to one scholarship recipient, and then afterwards opened to all eligible employees of his company. According to a letter from the university, my father was their first donor to choose this creative giving option."

His gift	$33,688
Capital gains savings	$6,490
Tax deduction savings	$8,000
Future income tax savings	$1,455
After tax income to student	$7,731
Total Family Benefit	**$23,676**

Essentially, it cost him $10,000 to make a $33,688 gift that created an endowed scholarship for his company's employees. That gift is still helping students today, nearly 30 years later.

Please humor me while I make something very clear. *Any time* that life insurance is considered as part of a gift planning strategy, it behooves all involved for your donor to put a policy in place and in force, with premiums paid, *before* any part of this solution is implemented. The reasons are self-evident: What if your donor is not insurable? Or the cost of the policy exceeds the economic benefit gained?

Having said that, on a Return on Investment basis, occasionally life insurance will earn a better return than traditional investments. The problem is, someone's gotta *die* to get the best results. As you can see, there is a built-in downside to winning this way. As a cancer survivor, I highly discourage it. In the early 1990's, I had a client visiting London for the weekend. He looked the wrong way when he crossed the street. To this day, "hit by a bus" is a phrase I avoid, and it's a lesson I will never forget.

WHAT ARE YOU GOING TO ASK FOR · 239

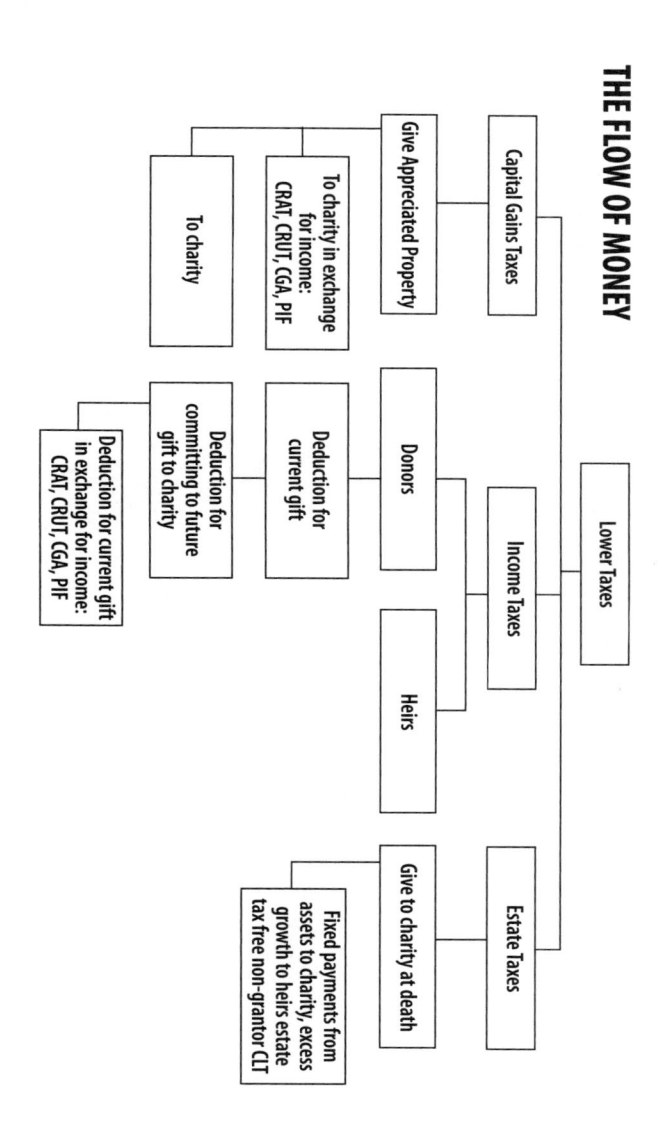

THE FLOW OF MONEY

- **Lower Taxes**
  - **Capital Gains Taxes**
    - Give Appreciated Property
      - To charity in exchange for income: CRAT, CRUT, CGA, PIF
      - To charity
  - **Income Taxes**
    - Donors
      - Deduction for current gift
      - Deduction for committing to future gift to charity
        - Deduction for current gift in exchange for income: CRAT, CRUT, CGA, PIF
    - Heirs
  - **Estate Taxes**
    - Give to charity at death
      - Fixed payments from assets to charity, excess growth to heirs estate tax free non-grantor CLT

A GIFT ACCEPTANCE POLICY WILL HELP YOU GRACIOUSLY SAY, "NO THANKS".

Policies and Procedures

A friend of mine was raised by two maiden aunts after his mother died in childbirth. (He has never discussed his father, and I never pushed it.) The second aunt died at age 103. The family farm was five states away. He was working full-time and said that he didn't have the time to travel to deal with the tenant farmers, manage a yard sale, etc. I suggested he give the farm, the land, and the contents to his university. The school had the capacity to send a team to the farm, where it discovered that the contents of the home went back three generations and were the stuff of *Antique Road Show* dreams: Revolutionary and Civil War weapons, women's clothing that had been preserved in tissue, and sterling silver from the mid-19th century. The university sent a team of curators to inventory this valuable collection. What would have wound up in a yard sale is now housed in various museums.

The university did such a great job with his aunt's estate that my friend wrote his first ever will and estate plan, leaving it all to his alma mater. With the university's development staff assisting him with his estate planning, he decided on an annuity that provided him an income, tax benefits, and recognition, which he loved. He got to know the new professors in his former department, geology, which he said was a great joy. My friend is only 79 and still skis and plays racquetball, so the university might have to wait another 20 years for his entire estate, but if they steward him well he will recruit others to share in the joy.

Here is the question: If your nonprofit were left this kind of a complex gift, would you have the staff, the funds, and the bandwidth to take multiple trips, contact a range of appraisers, and negotiate the sale of valuable items? This is an issue that would have to go to the board. Large nonprofits, such as The Nature Conservatory, have a large team that is knowledgeable about gifts of land. Museums have the staff to evaluate artwork. You might have the skills on the board, but you are talking a large commitment of time and money.

This is the reason you need a gift acceptance policy that is right-sized for your organizational capacity. Receiving a bequest is a no-brainer. You say thank you, work with the family on how to honor the donor, and cash the check. Land, art, cars, shares in privately held corporations, and other valuables might be too complex for your organization.

It is difficult to turn down such gifts. Years ago, a man named Robert Dickey donated land in Costa Rica to the American 501(c)3, the Friends of the Eternal Rainforest. It was approximately 130 acres of hilly land from the beach to the top of a steep hill, with what some appraisers assumed was a million-dollar view. The land was nowhere near the rainforest. It was undeveloped with no running water or electricity. However, the land was beachfront and the views majestic. Through the years, the value of the land was calculated between $650,000 and $3.5 million. Every person who joined the board said, "Sell the land."

Great idea. The woman who had sold the land to Mr. Dickey, however, had died, and her son was selling parcels of the property. He believed it was his land and couldn't fathom that his mother would sell the land without his knowledge or permission. This small nonprofit was in for a fight, and an expensive one.

As their consultant, I was asked to recruit a Spanish-speaking attorney who understood international real estate law. How hard could that be? It turned out to be quite easy. I went to the Hispanic Chamber of Commerce and the St. Louis Bar Association, and the same name came up, Gonzalo Fernandez. I approached Gonz, and son of a gun, I not only got Gonz, but his wife Anne, an accountant and marketing professional who was passionate about the environment. They said they would serve on the board for one year. Eight years later, they finally term-limited off the board. With lawyers in Costa Rica and a crack American/Argentinian attorney, the title was finally clear.

Meanwhile, this small nonprofit was paying yearly taxes on the land. Various board members made it their personal mission to sell the land. Two small problems: It was not near a city and a real estate agent would have to drive several hours to take clients to visit the property. Also, there were people with machetes who did not want anyone on the land. This generous gift continues to be a drain both in terms of time and money and, in 12 years, has yet to be resolved.

When accepting the land, the board failed to appreciate that many European and Latin American countries have protective laws for squatters. Even when there was a clear title, the board grossly underestimated the time and energy it would take to protect the ownership rights from a steady stream of locals who wanted to claim a piece of the property. On one trip to survey the land, the executive director, Laurie Waller, a very pregnant Costa Rican attorney, Gonz, and several guards hiked the perimeter, which took five hours. The driver who dropped them off fled immediately. Between the Costa Rican sun, the insects and brambles, and having to wield machetes to forge a way forward, this was no walk in the park. When a second driver came to pick them up at a faraway location, he brought cold Gatorade. Gonz sighed and said it was the best drink he ever had.

The board also failed to appreciate the remoteness of the property. In the U.S., we think that beachfront property is a no-brainer to develop, but this was in the middle of nowhere. Clearly, a cautionary tale of an asset becoming a liability.

The next level

Create and adopt a gift acceptance policy (GAP). This policy doesn't have to be perfect or exhaustive; it might be imperfect and exhausting! But don't despair, there are boilerplates available. Just start with the basics, and over time you will refine and add to your policy as needed. Having a basic gift acceptance policy can also help if some day in the future an enterprising board member gets excited about taking on that gas station because it needs "a little fixing up and then might be worth millions." You can gently avoid this catastrophe without making your board member look bad.

A GAP is an important tool in your planned giving toolkit. There are more sophisticated tools, but none as foundational as a GAP. It may be that your organization already has a GAP for annual gifts and is only lacking the additional component of policies related to planned gifts.

If your organization has neither, I recommend reaching out to a great resource for all things nonprofit and legal: the Nonprofit Risk Management Association (www.nonprofitrisk.org). This will help you understand two important things; how GAPs can help when it comes to annual and planned gifts, and how the policies all work together to enhance and protect your organization.

Let's take a closer look at what a GAP is and how you create it:

- Who writes it?
- Who authorizes it?
- What's in it?

The easy answers are:

Q: Who writes it?
A: In mid-sized organizations the staff generally takes the lead in writing the bones of the policy. Reaching out to other nonprofits to share their policies is common

practice. You aren't sharing your donor information, just the policies by which you relate to those donors. This approach can be particularly helpful if you are also "borrowing from" an organization that your board members are also familiar with. For example, the executive director of the Wildlife Rescue Center borrowed policies and procedures from the St. Louis Zoo. After a few conversations with the Zoo's planned giving officers, the Wild Life Center learned what they did (and did not) need in their policy.

Q: Who authorizes it?
A: The board of directors

This should be easy if a committee of the board is part of this process. Occasionally, a board member will get so bogged down in the weeds of the language that s(he) starts to scare other board members. You know the one: S(he) begins every question with, "But what if this happens?" Or, "What if we're wrong about that?" Don't worry. Just make sure that you have fellow board members to help you champion this process. It usually doesn't take much for one board member to remind your resident fearmonger that it is okay not to cover every possible contingency, such as a large gift of livestock to a Manhattan-based charity or a military tank to a ballet company.

If you are a chapter organization, hopefully your mothership has boilerplate policies.

Q: What's in your planned giving policy?
A: Generally, the answer is to keep it simple.

Below are four examples of Gift Acceptance Policies provided by the Nonprofit Risk Management Center. I am also including their Gifts Generally Accepted Without Review as an added component to help you on your way.

Sample Gift Acceptance Policies

- Sample #1
  - [Name of Nonprofit] solicits and accepts gifts that are consistent with its mission and that support its core programs as well as special projects.
  - Donations and other forms of support will generally be accepted from individuals, partnerships, corporations, foundations, government agencies, or other entities, subject to the following limitations: a. [describe limitations here, such as delivered to the agency, new or nearly new condition, proof of ownership.]
  - Gifts of Real Property, Personal Property or Securities may only be accepted upon approval of the [name of appropriate reviewing body, such as the nonprofit's Finance Committee].

- Sample #2
  - [Organization Name] solicits and accepts gifts that are consistent with its mission. Donations will generally be accepted from individuals, part-

nerships, corporations, foundations, government agencies, or other entities, without limitations.
- During its regular fundraising activities, [Organization Name] will accept donations of money, real property, personal property, stock, and in-kind services.
- Certain types of gifts must be reviewed prior to acceptance due to the special liabilities they may pose for [Organization Name]. Examples of gifts that will be subject to review include gifts of real property, personal property, and securities.

- Sample #3 [in the format of a corporate resolution]
  - Whereas [Organization Name] actively solicits gifts and grants to further the mission of the organization,
  - Whereas there is the potential for controversy if certain gifts are accepted, the organization has adopted the following Gift Acceptance Policy: When considering whether to solicit or accept gifts, the organization will consider the following factors:
    - *Values*—Whether the acceptance of the gift compromises any of the core values of [Organization Name]
    - *Compatibility*—Whether there is compatibility between the intent of the donor and the organization's use of the gift
    - *Public Relationships*—Whether acceptance of the gift damages the reputation of [Organization Name]

- ***Primary Benefit***—Whether the primary benefit is to [Organization Name] versus the donor
- ***Consistency***—Whether the acceptance of the gift is consistent with prior practice?
- ***Form of Gift***—Whether the gift is offered in a form that [Organization Name] can use without incurring substantial expense or difficulty?
- ***Effect on Future Giving***—Will the gift encourage or discourage future gifts? All decisions to solicit and/or accept potentially controversial gifts will be made by the Executive Committee of the Board in consultation with the Executive Director. The primary consideration will be the impact of the gift on the organization.

- Sample #4
  - [Organization Name] solicits and accepts gifts for purposes that will help the organization further and fulfill its mission.
  - [Organization Name] urges all prospective donors to seek the assistance of personal legal and financial advisors in matters relating to their gifts, including the resulting tax and estate-planning consequences.
  - The following policies and guidelines govern acceptance of gifts made to [Organization Name] for the benefit of any of its operations, programs, or services.

- *Use of Legal Counsel*—[Organization Name] will seek the advice of legal counsel in matters relating to acceptance of gifts when appropriate. Review by counsel is recommended for:
  - Gifts of securities that are subject to restrictions or buy-sell agreements
  - Documents naming [Organization Name] as trustee or requiring [Organization Name] to act in any fiduciary capacity
  - Gifts requiring [Organization Name] to assume financial or other obligations
  - Transactions with potential conflicts of interest
  - Gifts of property which may be subject to environmental or other regulatory restrictions
- *Restrictions on Gifts*—[Organization Name] will not accept gifts that:
  - would result in [Organization Name] violating its corporate charter
  - would result in [Organization Name] losing its status as an IRC § 501(c)(3) not-for-profit organization, or are too difficult or too expensive to administer in relation to their value
  - would result in any unacceptable consequences for [Organization Name], or are for purposes outside [Organization Name]'s mission.

Decisions on the restrictive nature of a gift and its acceptance or refusal, shall be made by the Executive Committee, in consultation with the Executive Director.

Gifts Generally Accepted Without Review

Cash
- Cash gifts are acceptable in any form, including check, money order, credit card, or online payments. Donors wishing to make a gift by credit card must provide the card type (Visa, MasterCard, American Express, etc.), card number, expiration date, and name of the cardholder as it appears on the credit card.

Marketable Securities
- Marketable securities may be transferred electronically to an account maintained at one or more brokerage firms or delivered physically with the transferer's endorsement or signed stock power (with appropriate signature guarantees) attached. All marketable securities will be sold promptly upon receipt unless otherwise directed by [Name of Organization]'s Investment Committee. In some cases, marketable securities may be restricted, for example, by applicable securities laws or the terms of the proposed gift. In such instances, the decision whether to accept the restricted securities shall be made by the Executive Committee.

Bequests and Beneficiary Designations under Revocable Trusts, Life Insurance Policies, Commercial Annuities, and Retirement Plans
- Donors are encouraged to make bequests to [Organization Name] under their wills, and to name

[Organization Name] as the beneficiary under trusts, life insurance policies, commercial annuities, and retirement plans.

Charitable Remainder Trusts
- [Organization Name] will accept designation as a remainder beneficiary of charitable remainder trusts.

Charitable Lead Trusts
- [Organization Name] will accept designation as an income beneficiary of charitable lead trusts. Gifts Accepted Subject to Prior Review—certain forms of gifts or donated properties may be subject to review prior to acceptance. Examples include, but are not limited to:

Tangible Personal Property
- The Executive Committee shall review and determine whether to accept any gifts of tangible personal property in light of the following considerations:
  - Does the property further the organization's mission? Is the property useful for the organization's purposes?
  - Is the property readily marketable? Are there covenants, conditions, restrictions, reservations, easements, encumbrances, or other limitations associated with the property?
  - Are there carrying costs (including insurance, property taxes, mortgages, notes, or the like) or maintenance expenses associated with the prop-

erty? Does the environmental review or audit reflect that the property is in compliance with existing regulations?

Life Insurance
- [Organization Name] will accept gifts of life insurance where [Organization Name] is named as both beneficiary and irrevocable owner of the insurance policy. The donor must agree to pay, before due, any future premium payments owing on the policy.

Real Estate
- All gifts of real estate are subject to review by the Executive Committee. Prior to acceptance of any gift of real estate other than a personal residence, [Organization Name] shall require an initial environmental review by a qualified environmental firm. In the event that the initial review reveals a potential problem, the organization may retain a qualified environmental firm to conduct an environmental audit.

Gift Acceptance Letters

There is a lot of controversy about gift acceptance letters. Some donors find them intrusive. This is especially true when they are asked to send a copy of the will or trust that discusses the gift. Some even ask for social security numbers, which many years ago used to be on our driver's licenses and now, in the digital age, are considered highly personal. On the other hand, if the gift is for something the nonprofit's gift acceptance policy forbids or frowns on, asking for a gift acceptance letter tells the nonprofit you have a problem and can renegotiate the gift. Sometimes it is the difference between giving to a local branch of a charity or the national. This is especially true of organizations that have many branches such as the Boy Scouts, The Red Cross, The American Cancer Society etc.

There can also be repercussions when there is not a legal document specifying how the donor will be honored and for how long. A recent high-profile example is Avery Fisher Hall in New York. Four decades ago, the Hall was named after Avery Fisher after a $10.5 million-dollar gift. Today it needs approximately $500 million dollars in repairs. For 13 years, the Fisher family fought the change. There was no agreement as to how long the Hall would have the family name on it. It was finally settled with a payment of $15 million to the Fisher family, freeing the organization to sell the naming rights to David Geffen for $100 million.

Granted, these are sums that might not apply to your nonprofit, but the concept is the same. What does the donor expect from a major or planned gift and what is the nonprofit willing or able to do when the estate is executed?

Every gift acceptance letter should begin with a thank you. You will want the following information:

What kind of gift is it? Real estate, a percentage of the estate, a dollar amount, life insurance, etc.?

If the form attached to the letter is not signed, you will want to follow up with the donor and find out why. Normally, the letters state that the gift is not binding.

You might want to google "Gift Acceptance Letters" and find one that fits your organization. There are many examples that are Hemmingway simple or as clear as a Shakespearean sonnet to a non-English speaker. This is definitely a case of one size does not fit all. It is important to include the length of naming rights unless the gift is endowed. Forever is a long, long time and when you have facilities like a Boys and Girls Club or an orchestral hall that is heavily used, you can count on maintenance needs in the years to come, not to mention changes in the laws for facilities that require earth quake proofing, access for the disabled, sprinkler systems and countless other expensive upgrades. The ability to offer naming rights to another donor when the previous donor's naming has run out can make a huge difference in your ability to raise funds.

Summary

In short, the basic components of any gift acceptance policy are what types of gifts your organization can and will take, and under what conditions. Again, don't worry if your GAP does not capture everything. As your planned giving program grows, there will be more opportunities to revisit your policy and to ask if more gifts can be added.

Likewise, with your gift acceptance letter, listen to feedback from your donors. If your letters are not returned, you have a clear indication you are asking for the wrong information or too much information and need to revamp the letter. For complex gifts with naming rights and endowments, you will need to hand craft the letter rather than using a template.

"FOR THAT SIZE DONATION, THE HOSPITAL SAYS WE CAN NAME A PAPER CUP DISPENSER, OR A MAGAZINE RACK."

12

The power phrases that pay

I was teaching a group of doctors involved in a capital campaign how to ask for a gift. The chair of breast cancer surgery said, "It is really hard to talk about money." I asked her when her last do-not-resuscitate conversation was. She looked down and said, "This morning." I asked the group how they learned to have difficult conversations. They told tales of horrific behavior, which they pledged never to repeat, as well as kind methods of delivering bad news, which they tried to emulate. I asked what was the difference between their early days as interns and now. The breast cancer surgeon said, "I know what to say. I can focus on the patient and family and not think about what I am going to say next."

The same is true of asking for a planned gift. The more you do it, the less you think about what you are going to say next, and the more you focus on the donor.

I wanted to leave you with some phrases that might help.

From the solicitor to the donor
- Please join me as a legacy donor
- You can change the future
- You can make a difference
- You can expand the influence of
- If you could restrict your planned gift to a specific service of XYZ, what would that be?
- You can help to eliminate
- Without your help

Or consider this approach: "We just received a generous planned gift to support the work you have been funding. If you would like to talk about doing the same and joining this donor in saving even more children/ dogs/ land, etc., I'd love to share what changes we could make."

- Together we will be able to
- What a wonderful way to honor your wife, sister, or father
- I love the way you are approaching your estate plan. I am going to consider that possibility myself.

"Giving phrases" to listen for from your donor
- I wish I could do more
- I would like to see a future without
- I would like my grandchildren to live in a world where

- There is one thing that is still on my bucket list that I haven't been able to check off
- If only I could go back and
- If only your services had been available when I was younger
- I owe my life to your staff
- It disturbs me that more people don't have access to
- I want to recognize the caregiver who helped us so much
- It's terrible that some people in our community have to travel so far to receive care
- How could I ever repay your organization

Final thoughts:

Never forget the most common reason that people don't give is that they are not asked. If they say no, be gracious. If they say yes, steward them like mad.

Acknowledgments

It may take a village to raise a child, but for me to write a book takes a whole lot more people.

My first thank you is to my editor, Cheryl Jarvis. I met Cheryl in 1986 when she interviewed me for an article in *St. Louis* magazine about families raising children without a TV. Thanks to Cheryl, I was on Oprah, who did very well after I was on her show. My only regret is that I never got to say, "It is great to be back to tell you about my new book." Cheryl's world and mine collide in many ways. Her mother was my husband's French teacher, her brother lived down the street, and my son babysat for her nephew. Once a week, she walks me around Forest Park. We look like a Great Dane and a Chihuahua. She is a gracious and diligent writing teacher and a *New York Times* bestselling author who continues to patiently instruct me in the art of parallel construction and when not to capitalize the words 'Mother" and "Board."

My peer review committee, which made numerous suggestions that helped immensely, includes: Bill Beggs, Stan Coffman, Susan Ellis, Larry Katzenstein, Nina Needleman, Larry Levin, and Steven Shattuck.

Special thanks to the generosity of Russell James, Stanley Weinstein, Vanessa K. Bohns who gave me permission to share their knowledge. I feel ridiculous calling these superstars my colleagues. I am a pipsqueak compared to them.

None of this book would be possible without my amazing clients. How many people can say that everyone they work with wants to make the world a better place? Plus, I am old enough and cranky enough that if I don't like someone, I won't work with them, so I wind up adoring all my clients. They share their stories, their trials, their sleepless nights, their knowledge, and their passion. I am grateful for their confidences.

My favorite two hours of my professional life occur during the Nonprofit Leadership Forum. I have up to eight CEOs meet in my office as a mastermind group to brainstorm. We started in 2012. Three are now consultants, several have stayed for years, and all share their incredible expertise.

I also want to acknowledge my consultants' group. We meet for two days several times a year to discuss our practices and our challenges and to establish priorities for the future. Michael Daigneault, Cris Wineinger, Kenny Sigler, Marilyn Abegg, Rachel Muir, Rick Moyers and Patrick Willis.

ACKNOWLEDGMENTS · 265

Peggy Nehmen was my savior and the shepherd of this book. She designed the cover, the pagination, held my hand and listened to me whine. If she gets bored with the book biz, she can always become a therapist or get some real sheep and become a shepherdess.

Michael and Mary McMurtrey, you hopefully know how I appreciate all of your guidance, support and help.

A special thanks to my dear friend Tom Bakewell. I love working with you, even if there is almost nothing we agree on. You are a terrific friend, colleague and mentor.

Dennis Fletcher has been my cartoonist for years. He is triple funny: With his cartoons, in e-mails and on the phone. I really must meet him someday.

And, as always, thanks to the love of my life, Frank Robbins, the senior vice president of schlepping and my husband for more since 1976. He's always supportive, always kind, and always willing to get me a latte.

Thank you for reading this book...

If you are looking for a motivational keynote, a facilitator for a retreat or a workshop on how to ask for a major, capital or planned gift or just need to get your board to understand their roles and responsibilities, please call me at 314 863 4422, e-mail me at Carol@BoardBuilders.com or check out my website www.BoardBuilders.com.

Raising Charitable Children, based on my book by the same name, is also a popular topic. This topic has been particularly popular with community foundations, the clients of wealth advisors, places of worship and schools.

What makes me unique? I believe I am the only fundraising speaker who has also done stand-up comedy. I can also tap dance... badly, but I keep taking lessons. If AARP revises "A Chorus Line," I will be ready.

If you are interested in bulk sales of 10 copies or more of any of my books for your entire team or donors, please contact Board Builders directly.

And finally, this book is outdated the day it goes to press. The laws changed dramatically while writing this tomb and they will continue to change. If there are changes that you are aware of, please let me know and I can incorporate them immediately in the downloadable version.

Again, thanks for the work you do. And thank you for reading this book.

       Fondly,
       Carol